MW01030805

Conquering Domestic Violence

Dr. Horace Morson

PRESS

Conquering Domestic Violence
by Dr. Horace Morson

Printed in the United States of America

ISBN 9781628390964

www.xulonpress.com

Contents

Dedication vii

Chapter I

Conquering at the root 12
Domestic violence in the past versus the present 17
Children having children 23
Factors that influence Domestic Violence 31
Stop getting involved so soon 38
Lock a Dollar up 41
Don't be to quick to assume 44
Step Children should respect Step Parents 48

Chapter II

An honest Amnesty Program 52
Testimonies 56
Form a Supporting Cast 61
Decision making Exercise 64
Extinguish the Silence 67
Education at all Channels 71

Chapter III

Practicing Independence 75
Stopping Compulsory Relationship Disorder 78

Some tips to Help 82
Some ways infatuation works 87
Pull down the Bar 89
A better funding Program 92
Volunteer your service 96
Change your Hang out Crowd 100
Defeating the intimidation of Weapons 104
Break down the Walls 107
Consult the Family 110
Off the record Child-Support 112
Conquering setups for Abuse 115
Learn to Cope 117
Should his child ride in another mans car 120
Discourage Laboring for Government Benefits 123
Boot Camp will give you some ideas 126
Men must report it 129
A tour of the Body 130
Close the Gap 132
More Accountability 137
Reduce the case Load 140

Part II

Chapter IV

Can Religion do It 145
Global Awareness 149
Keep the Children Safe 150
Revoke the weapon Licenses 150
Report Suspicious Stalkers 151
What the future Holds 151
Conclusion 154

Dedication

This Book is dedicated to all the families whose lives have being disrupted by Domestic Violence but especially to those who have loss love ones as a result of Domestic Violence. May I say to everyone, the battle of this violence is still raging but the spirit to conquer rest with within you.

Chapter I

Conquering Domestic Violence

Introduction

In the last decade, domestic violence has been on the increase. It has become everyone's business and has touched every class and every color and reached every place. It's now carried out in all form and fashion among all ages and is not limited to any particular gender. The word *violence* may sometimes be used instead of the word *abuse*, but in any event, whichever word is used, the underlying act is brutal and inhumane behavior among families that causes critical pain and sometimes death.

The violence has caused many groups, analysts, domestic violence lawyers, and different programs to rise up from all over the globe, but in spite of all these proactive personnel and agencies, domestic violence keeps climbing and spreading to places where it is least expected. It is like wildfire. If we could put our finger on its pulse, we would have it under control by now, but because its approach is different in every culture, it gets to be very difficult to stop. Therefore, every possible aggressive measure must be taken to conquer this beast.

There is nothing beautiful in watching a young lady with her face all twisted out of shape with colors black and blue around her eyes, beaten by some man whom she called her boyfriend or husband. Or covering her eyes with sunglasses since they are so red and swollen, because she cried all night in anguish and pain for abusive treatment she received from the man in her life.

There is no beauty in watching a hard-working responsible man walking down the street with his hair as nappy as wool and his face as sad as doomsday because the lady in his life constantly takes his wages and gives him the boot to the street, telling him always he is a loser and a good-for-nothing.

There is nothing great about parents slapping their children up against their heads, putting bruises on their bodies, and sending them off to school in the name of strict discipline. Abuse, domestic violence— whichever name you choose; it really doesn't matter for all of it adds up to pain—and pain that is done by people who are supposed to be significant figures in these victims' lives.

The injury involved in domestic violence is not always physical; sometimes it is emotional and leads to depression and other psychological and social dysfunctions, such as anxiety and social isolation or even suicide. This type of violence can devastate an entire family and cause trust to be lost in society. Some Scientists for many years have carried out research on various project in their particular field of study, but became discourage because of very little progress made. It is quite possible that this attitude could be taken against domestic crime and would make all the efforts in fighting against it become just a "going through the motion" type of fight, with hardly any passion to control it. If we approach it this way, more than likely it will be seen that way, and the battle will be lost. Let us face the fact that domestic crime already exists before we were born and will be after we are gone. In the meantime we must think of our children and our children's children, who will be affected by the crime with very few weapons to fight with if we do not make any effort to conquer it now. We must take into consideration that the crime is not bigger than us as humans; we are the vehicle for the crime, and if the vehicle can be altered, then the crime will become disabled. With all the other different tools used in other warfare today, one of the best ways to conquer domestic crime is to be proactive in preparing the weapons or defense against the crime, rather than to be reactive after the crime is committed.

This approach must be a committed one that involves parents, schools, religion or other organizations, government agencies, outreach program activities, and other related affiliations. Whenever and wherever domestic violence is addressed or discussed, emphasis on conquering the crime should be expressed rather than just lamenting its existence and calling it a day. If we look on domestic crime lightly, our own sons and daughters could become caught up into it; therefore a passion to conquer it should always be a drive in our heart.

With a passion to conquer it, we will save lives, and the life that we save could be our own.

Conquering At The Root

Domestic violence should not surprise anyone as though it is something that fell out of the sky and all of a sudden began to take over our society. It's not. It has its history. It started in the biblical days with two brothers, Cain and Abel, when one killed the other because there was a jealousy of the sacrifice offered to God by the elder brother. Then later on during enslavement, we notice that because of the pressure that slaves were receiving on the field and in the slave masters' houses, working without being paid, slaves would then go home to their own families after their tasks were over with their masters and abuse members of their families out of anger, venting in the wrong way. Moving from slavery to the medieval ages, we again find that many women of that age, especially many years following the Roman Empire, were exploited by their husbands and other men on certain festive occasions. During these occasions, these women were known to prepare food for the festivities and after the preparation, they were supposed to get back to their places in their homes while the men enjoy the festivals. If a wife was seen anywhere in the festival

12

room among any of the men, she would be beaten furiously by her husband in an abusive manner.

On the other hand on some occasions in the festivity (certain festivity) one or two women would be brought to the festival to dance and perform before all the men, after which they would be sexually abused and sometimes raped.

There is absolutely no doubt that these crimes are not yesterday's crimes, but yesteryears' crimes, and one of the reason why they prevailed so long is because of cultural tolerance from generation to generation.

It would only be crippling of the mind to believe that because domestic violence has been around for a long time and that some cultures have tolerated it for so long that it will be very difficult to get rid of it. I would love to believe that we can stamp it out completely, but unfortunately I cannot, because from day to day our generation changes. As we become more exposed to different environments, we become more aggressive and retaliate. However, taking all things into consideration, I believe that as a civilized generation we can grab the bull by the horns and take the necessary steps to meet the crime at its potential starting point, that is, at the root—the young men and women that will grow up to wrestle with it in the future.

Can you imagine what it would be like if every tree that is now fully grown in strength was allowed to grow wildly on its own without the proper nurturing and care from its root such as watering, nutrients, and perhaps protection from being trampled upon by animals and other creatures? It would not be surprising to know that if that was the case, all around us where we live would look like a deserted forest of crooked-looking trees. Fortunately that is not the case because specialists such as horticulturists take time to care for the young plant so that they can grow up into tall strong trees.

Let me suggest that we learn a lesson from the plant or tree that was only six inches tall and is now twenty feet in the air to be able to understand how we can conquer domestic violence in our youth before they become victims and victimizers of it. There are certain functions about a child that are involuntary at birth through life, such as certain muscle movement, yawning, eye blinking, and bathroom habits and such. These are movements and responses of the nervous system. Meanwhile there are some other habits and actions that are not involuntary but rather are adopted or contracted, such as certain aggression, anger, stubbornness, and resentfulness. You may argue the statement of saying that these behaviors contain the hidden seed of domestic violence if not carefully dealt with. We must never dismiss the idea of a hidden seed with a potential to be devastating rests in every child, or we will lose the battle right there because we either take things for granted or live in denial. Whether or not that seed is in the child's genes (as some may argue) or it's picked up from the child's environment,it is a seed that will blossom and perhaps bear fruit in the future. The question we will now ask is, what kind of fruit will come from that seed? Would it be one that is a culprit of domestic violence? That we do not know, but what we do know is that when certain aggressive violent behavior is found in a youth who is the root of tomorrow's tree, actions are imminent.

With a mindset to conquer domestic violence from its roots (the young children), parents, guardians, and all those who stand before young children every day in different capacities must study these children diligently and work graciously with all wisdom to help them channel their behavior without being physical when they get upset, feel disappointed, ready to throw temper tantrums, or feel like they lost control.

The parents, guardians, and figures of authority must make sure that they work to cultivate acceptable habits and behaviors that they see in children, in order to have a brighter tomorrow and a much more reasoning and nonviolent society. It is at the root that all is formulated, and knowing that a tree begins from its root, it is logical to say that whatever is fed in the root will be manifested in the branch. Children therefore need the right nurturing, the right training, and the right discipline to help them through life. Not just a brand named shoe or shirt.

Domestic violence will never be conquered if there is no discipline and no boundaries given in early life. Domestic violence will never be conquered if the roots (children) are not taught the true value and appreciation of their lives and the lives of others. Love, value, and appreciation for others and themselves must be instilled in young children like having a three-course meal and monitoring to make sure that it becomes a part of their lifestyle. Such habits must be strongly enforced by those who watch over them in whatever capacity they serve. There should be absolutely no room for error because the terror of domestic violence is growing at a rapid pace but can slow down if it's battled early at the root—the young ones who will be tomorrow's husbands and wives, uncles and aunts, nieces and nephews.

We have pinpointed a place to start, but that's not all that is needed at the root to fight this battle and become conquerors. We must also keep in mind that everyone involved in combat must be trained before they go on the battlefield. No one fights just for fighting. I suppose that everyone fights to win. It is possible to fight and win if what we are supposed to be fighting against is also what we practice. How could someone teach against alcohol when the teacher is a strong alcoholic? It doesn't work that way; it's a conflict.

Conquering domestic violence at the root would also mean therefore that those who are the figureheads monitoring and enforcing workable behaviors in children must practice what they preach. That is, they must not exhibit poor and violent behaviors in the presence of children and at the same time expect to train the children to keep out of violent behaviors. This is not only conflicting but confusing at the roots.

The mission is to train, cultivate, and educate at the roots so that domestic violence can be eradicated early. This mission must be clear, and the soldiers (teachers, parents, etc.) must be equipped and not have a double standard. When everything is organized to work the way it is expected to, we can look towards the next ten to twelve years where we will see a great reduction in the rate of domestic violence because that generation would have been curtailed at their roots before they become trees.

The battle at the root may be a tough one, but with commitment, consistency, and a passion to conquer, we all together can get it done. So let us all get to work at the roots now.

Domestic Violence In The Past
Versus The Present

Domestic violence always carries a venom and a devastating force behind it, but in the past, although that was known to be, many people went to bed with it. In other words, as crucial as it was it was a violence that they were willing to live with as a part of life. During that era, women were mostly the victims of violence and still are. Many women were beaten badly by their husband or boyfriends, but refused to make a big deal out of it because doing so would cause them to lose their mate and leave them semi-domestically paralyzed.

It was internationally known that in the very early centuries, many women were not out in the work force; it was just a limited number because the traditional belief was that the women must stay at home while the men go to work. This type of climate positions women to lean on their husbands and boyfriends as the sole dependent and therefore forces them to accept all kind of abusive treatment and violent behaviors. Many women were beaten so badly by their spouse that they turned to alcohol to drown their grief and pain, and then later died from alcoholic related health issues as a result of long periods of abuse. Other women were so frequently beaten by their spouse that they become addicted to the abuse and at times felt that if their husband did not beat them, it meant that the husband did not love them. There were also times when the women had to go through a "bittersweet moment": that is, they were beaten and abused one moment and then enjoyed intimacy a few minutes later. The constant pattern of abuse and domestic violence was frequent, the pain and cry of victims were loud, but very little attention was given to the cry. On very few occasions the police would be called, and when they did come, they would only try to appease the situation because their hands were tied as far as how far they could go with domestic abuse. There were laws and punishments just for domestic violence, but the enforcement by the courts were weak. Therefore, men kept on doing what they were doing to women because they knew that the consequences were really a slap on the wrist.

However dark those days were, the women who were abused and were victims of domestic violence have caused some attention to be drawn to their treatment ,and as a result, new and stronger laws against domestic violence internationally are now in place. Whereas in the past verbal and mental abuse were looked upon as simple infractions, today there are serious cases of domestic violence. The awareness of the violence is on high alert, and more often than before, advocates against domestic violence as well as different types of educational programs against domestic violence are popping up all over the globe. Frankly, victims and potential victims have more tools to work with today to reduce the crime than ever before and therefore must use them. Even in some schools, domestic violence prevention programs find a place in the curriculum. It can never be emphasized enough of the large support given by foundational groups and active organizations to programs that are fighting this type of violence. Many supports from churches to nonprofit organizations, various government agencies, individual support, as well as private support have been also given to the fighters against domestic violence. It's overwhelming to see how strong the support to fight against domestic violence is, yet despite such support all over the world, domestic violence is still on the rise. This only says that there is an area or areas that the advocates have not yet touch or if they have, they may have to revisit those areas and check off what they did not do when they went there.

I don't mind saying that sometimes some of the things that we want most will mean giving up some of the things that we love best. To have quality life means to make great sacrifice, and if something is worth living for, it is also worth suffering ridicule for. This means that if we really want to conquer domestic violence, we will have targeted some of the perpetrators such as the film industry with movies magnifying domestic violence. How can we fight against something one day and be entertained by it the next day? It's nothing but a conflict. We must make a decision of what we honestly want to do. How could we have our families and friends sit back and watch a movie portraying domestic violence but fighting against it at the same time? I hope that you can find courage to continue to read this book; however I must tell you that the battle of winning or losing is in the mind, and whatever a person absorbs consistently and regularly will become a part of them sooner or later. If one sits around and is entertained by movies that will encourage domestic violence, whether on a mild scale or extreme scale, they will later rise up to practice what they have been watching, for we are creatures that are built to put out only what we take in. I am fully aware that many may say, "It's only a movie; don't take it so serious." Yes I am aware that it's a movie, but the brain is processing all the actions, and once it gets there in the brain, it stays there until the fullness of time.

I am not suggesting that anyone should tie a sheet over the face of their television and don't watch it at any time; neither am I suggesting that you should dump your DVD player or such. My point is that one of the ways to start conquering domestic violence is to make choices of the movies you rent or buy for entertainment. If they promote domestic violence then they should be inappropriate to watch and should be out of your possession. You may in some respect reduce the market for this product; whether you do or not, the fact is you do not control the production of the product, but you control what comes to you and your household and when you choose to eliminate from your possession promotional audio items of domestic violence, you have taken a step to conquer domestic violence. You then have saved the life of someone.

In the early centuries domestic violence was a cause of concern to the communities, but was very much down played because there was not too much media attention given to it. However, in the late nineteenth century much greater concern has been given to the violence because of its activity increase. These increases have come about by the more accessibility that people now have in promoting the violence. Some of these accessibilities are modern technology that people have to encourage and plan the violence, more freedom of traveling from one country to another, which could be held as getaway sports for a long time after a committed crime, and more time to stalk someone because of social freedom.

I don't want anyone to believe that these accessibilities cause domestic violence. They do not; they are just vehicles or avenues that are used to enhance the violence. The question that may now be asked is, "Because of these accessibilities that are now available, does that mean that people should stop traveling to other countries and get rid of modern technology such as Internet service, iPods, and cellphones with cameras and other devices?" Should people not enjoy their social freedom? That's not at all the suggestion I am making, for all of them have their place, especially in our modern society. The way I strongly urge to help conquer domestic violence is to use these same accessibilities to work against the act. For instance, whoever is a victim of domestic violence should use the Internet discretely to tell their story or experience and share tips to others to help them to get out of abusive situations and also to let others know how you got into it. Because the Internet is where ninety-eight percent of the world goes for information, the experience or story will appear to the international population, and whether or not we want to accept it, there will be someone dealing with the same experience that will be helped by Internet broadcast. That person may not necessarily be living within your own state or country or may not even speak your language. Nevertheless that piece of information may help them to free themselves from the bondage of domestic violence. In the case of traveling and interacting with others, that something that cannot stopped because human beings are social interactive creatures. The caution that I would give is not to be so ready to have a comfort level with someone who you do not know. Just because they are popular, they are financially stable, or they are known to have close ties with people of significant status in office does not necessarily make them cute. These are the people who are more likely to be domestically violent with you, for they tend to believe that they are above the law because of status and association; therefore they treat you like an object and not like a human being.

Too often, males and females meet each other at parties and functions, on trains and buses, don't know anything about each other, have not taken the time to know anything about each other, but fall into intimate relationships with promises that never get fulfilled and then later fall into domestic disputes and violence. The question asked is what must we do because we have needs that need to be met?

I understand that it is a concern that many people have today, but I must also say to you that to conquer domestic violence is not to allow your needs and desires to dictate your quality of life. If you keep falling for everyone that passes your way because of your needs and desires, you could be falling into the hands of domestically violent people, and because you are with them for the wrong reason, it becomes very easy for either one to become violent to the other. What's needed is a quality relationship, which comes with patience and time and also details screening of individuals to the best of your knowledge. With proper detail screening, any hidden agenda will manifest itself and potential domestic violence could be stomped before it moves into a relationship to become statistics.

In other words conquer domestic violence not with the words on" I Love You ,lets go out" but with"I have to know more about you, I am not taking what you are telling me." My friends, time changes, and so do men. The things of the past are not the same as the present things. Try to control the impulsive feeling that you may have from time to time, and by exercising self-control over your sexual appetite you will conquer possible domestic violence that was heading your way.

Children Having Children

It's heartbreaking enough to watched adults in their thirties, forties, and fifties going in and out of shelters where they have little or no privacy and a place where they have to run to, to rescue their lives from abusive violent spouses and mates. But it's even more troubling to see young adults eighteen, nineteen, and early twenties crawling in and out of shelters for the battered because they find themselves in abusive and violent relationships.

What might be some of the reasons? Today's generation is a very liberal and promiscuous one, one in which youths are very much out of control. We are faced with the unfortunate situations of many young people dropping out of school at a very early age, young people with very strong addiction habits, as well as young boys and girls who live in their parents' house and got their parents sanction to bring in that home their little girlfriend and boyfriend or several of them. I could say quite a bit on the school dropouts and the addictions, but let me spend some time talking about the issues of boyfriends and girlfriends' coming to parents' home since home is where everything begins. We will never be able to conquer domestic violence if we do not come to grips with the truth that some of the contributors to the violence are parents who will not lead by example and parents who will not set a standard for the home.

We must never forget that children copy what they see and also internalize what they feel most of the time. All or most children at an early age know the status of their parents, they know whether they are married or not, they also know who is and who is not their father or mother, they know when they see a different face (whether it is male or female) every other week in their home, they know something is not right, and they develop a suspicion eventually. Now you may say that the children ought to know their place in such homes and say nothing in regards to what they see because they are not paying any of the bill in the house; therefore, they have no say with what you do; they should "just put up and shut up." Of course they may put up but not shut up, or they may shut up but not put up. They are going to react in some way to what they feel because their space is being invaded. Some of the ways in which they may react is by picking fights with their siblings of the opposite sex because they are trying to express the anger they feel for the environment that they are forced to live in, and as a result of the constant bickering, one of the individual involved could find themselves prematurely into the domain of a young male or female partner their age, to soon learn that he or she will be a parent at an early age. This happens because the home becomes disrupted by a disrespectful parent.

On the other hand not all young people respond to a disrupted home that way; there are those children who use their parents' practice as a comfort zone for them to bring the little girlfriend or boyfriend in the home, and in some situations some parents tolerate it because they cannot tell the child it is wrong, for they themselves are doing the same thing, and a pot cannot tell the kettle that it is black. We do not have to ask the outcome of such calamity, for we can be assured that it will also be that premature parents are getting ready to give birth to innocent babies.

How troubling is this in reference to domestic violence? In the case where the upset of the home causes siblings to pick fights with each other only sets the stage for early practice of fighting at home. It could be a brother fighting with his sister or the sister with the brother; whichever way it goes, it is low level domestic violence to become full blown in future relationships. Once this is embedded into youths it becomes a part of the foundational upbringing and later on carry over to adult life as the individuals tries to settle down to live with someone.

It is a known fact that about nine out of every ten children that grow up in an outstandingly poor environments make extremely poor choices in life that impact their future. This kind of lifestyle allows victims of such environments to fall into relationships early with all the anger and disappointments of home, and out of these relationships children are born of parents that have no clue of responsibilities or parenting. It's moments and occasion like these that domestic violence are in bed with the couples, waiting for an explosion because the understanding of parenting and domestic responsibilities have never really being addressed and dealt with prior to making a family, so when the family begins to form, the pressure of responsibilities compounded with the anger and disappointments that were already there presents nothing less than domestic violence as the product.

There isn't any benefit in saying, "Well there is nothing we can do about that to each his own, as we always say," or even to say "People make their own choices of what they want to do." That's understood, but our world is getting overrun with domestic violence in all age groups, all cultures, and all races because of the lack of guidance. We now need to pull out all the conquering power tools that we can find, or else we will live to regret that we didn't do anything for our sons and daughters to help them through life.

Here are some conquering tools that we can use in this particular situation of children having children:

*Parents should take some time out to explain to their children the difficulties that come with being parents early. They should, in an educational manner, share some of their early life experience with their children and the struggles they faced in premature family planning if that's the case. They should not hide any conflicts that they feel could have escalated into domestic violence from their children but should let them know how they were able to avoid it or prevent the thought of domestic violence. Although times have changed and the generation is different, such education, especially from parents, will help the children to reflect back before they encounter such situation or in the situation.

*Fathers should take their son aside, and mothers take their daughters routinely and teach them how to reason in conflicting times without becoming verbally and physically abusive in any way. In fact all parents should first live this life before their children before they could introduce it to their children. If parents introduced this to their children and don't live it, the counsel will never be taken seriously by the children. It would be a good idea for both parents to put their respective children through the test on different occasions with different cultures and correct them to help

27

them because one never knows the culture or race that their child will become the husband or wife of.

*Apart from what parents should do, there should be some kind of mandatory domestic violence prevention program done in all schools as part of the curriculum. This is important because before children move on to college to further their education the last educational institution of their early life is high school and this is where many of them begin their relationships with the man or woman that they will marry and make a family with in the future. Therefore a domestic prevention program as part of their high school education can make a great difference.

These ideas are not to make anyone feel irresponsible in any way, but we must understand that when anything we deal with is getting out of control, we will use every tool necessary to get it back in line. We can never be naïve about domestic violence. It's on the increase, and every measure must be taken to control it before it controls the lives of our future sons and daughters.

Hands Off Heads On:

The actions taken by one's hands are the results of decisions made by the brain. Whether or not those decisions are positive or negative, offensive or defensive, they are what the brain tell us to do to resolve matters. Now we must understand that some of these reactive decisions are instant reactions and some take time to be carried out, but the fact is the hand and every other part of the body are not independent, and by themselves they can only do what the brain tells them to do at the moment. No form of domestic violence really makes sense except it's in self-defense, but during the ages we have encountered some domestic violence, which tells us that the hands of the perpetrators were completely out of control.

There seems to be a misunderstanding among individuals of what the hands were made for. Far too many people misused their hands. For instance, it becomes easier for a person to slap another person than to use the hand and drive a nail with a hammer in a wall. It becomes easier for the hands to rip the clothes off of another than to wash them and iron them for the same person. I will not hesitate to say that the hand has become a destructive force and is a major weapon in carrying out domestic violence. It's in the hands that guns and knives are placed for criminal actions; it's in the hands that tools are given to break down doors for the force entry into someone's apartment to do harm. If we stop and evaluate for a minute we can conclude that, yes the brain will continue to make decisions that could be painful to others, but pain cannot be inflicted unless actions are carried out especially with the hand not involved.

The concern now before us is how domestic violence can be conquered by the hand. The answer is use the hand for the purpose it was created for and the brain for the same purpose. That is, they both were created to help, not to destroy.

Quite often we do walk into provocation, or sometimes it comes to our door without invitation. Quite often couples living together experience conflicts that eventually end up into brawls. During these times the normal response is the temptation of using offensive words followed by physical attacks by the hand that can be extremely dangerous for either party. Before the situation gets to this level, it would be better for one of the parties to reverse the negative impulses that he is having from his brains, turn them into something positive by either viewing the conflict differently or finding other constructive ways of infiltrating the conflict to prevent any rage or physical abuse that leads to domestic violence. This may mean that someone would have to leave the scene for a moment to avoid a rage. However, though this may be necessary at the time if it has to be done, it must be done in a manner of respect to the problem and to the other person involved. This should not be done in a rage, but with diligence and understanding. Never should it be interpreted that walking away for a moment is defeat on one's behalf, it's not as a matter of fact, and it's a shot in the leg on domestic violence because it's finding an intelligent way to resolve a conflict without any physical or verbal harm. Often times when there is a reentry of two people to readdress a conflict, the conflict becomes easier to resolve without the unnecessary provocation of words or attitudes.

The walk may involve a social moment at one of the in-laws home. This becomes helpful because the moment helps to discourage any thought of inflicting pain and encourages a closer bond with the family members so by the time the individuals return to their own home, a much friendlier environment exists and the chance of potential conflict is reduced. The goal in all of this is to keep the hand in disciplinary cus-tody and the brain in the right gear: that is to reason, resolve, and bring closure to any provoking domestic violence action. The hand in action versus the brain at work is a battle that every married couple and every family member battles with quite often, and depending on which one we listen to will be the one that wins. It doesn't really matter what gender you are . What matters is that if everyone uses their head in an anti-violence manner, domestic violence will experience its divorce in the lives of many, and good relationships will sit in the driver's seat. Domestic violence is a fast moving crime all over the world; therefore, we must all adjust ourselves to use our head and not our hand to conquer this crime, for it awaits every color, sex, class, or creed in their own life and in their homes but could be buried by the brain.

Factors That Influence Domestic Violence

Expectation:

We were all created with imperfection, and none of us will ever be the perfect man or woman that we desire to be, for we are just not wired that way. However, we strive to be our best, but what is the best to us is not enough for others. Every horse does not run at the same pace and therefore will not reach to the finish line at the same time, but they all can reach it if they continue to run to achieve. I am more than willing to believe that one of the reasons for domestic violence is that too many times in relationships, one party expects too much of the other and expects it instantly . When such is the environment, frustration sets in followed by negative attitudes, comments, and behaviors that invite domestic violence. It is a sure fact that every individual has their own unique qualities and their own unique weakness, but despite those weaknesses, all still need work to be done to themselves. Some may need work to develop good qualities while others may need work only to maintain the good qualities that are already developed. Nevertheless, whether it's a little work or a considerable amount of work, it's still work; therefore, no one should look for perfection in the other.

When you chose to be in a marital relationship, you did not marry the skeleton of your spouse; you married the sum total of the man or woman—that is, the individual and all that comes with their person. If later in life you feel your expectations are not met, do not become frustrated and begin a critical game, for it's things like that breed the entrance of domestic violence. Instead, turn your disappointments into some positive actions and do some things that are supportive.

Offering support to someone with deficiencies is a way of conquering domestic violence. People who have setbacks in their lives are already not too happy themselves and do not need to become more unhappy by having someone, constantly beating them in their aching spot, thinking that it will be make them better. They are looking for help and support. You may think that deep in the hearts of tough men and strong women there is not a little boy or a little girl crying out for help but you are wrong, for there is a cry, and this cry when not resolved results in anger, which is one of the elements of domestic violence.

The way you can help your spouse is not to approach his or her deficiencies with disgust or anger, but assure them that although you are not the one with the deficiency, you feel as though you are because you both are one. Assure them that you are all in this together and you will adjust yourself as much as possible to work with them so that you both can get through the setbacks whatever they are. Do not at any time put the spouse in a position to feel insignificant and useless, but let your support be one that gives them confidence and hope. Keep in mind that you are that person's partner, and they look to you for approval, so your support must be diligent yet still with no compromise. If you emotionally abandon them because of their setbacks, you may be only putting coals in a fire that is already burning and could be violent. The best solution for fire is water, so don't live with too many expectations of your spouse; he/she is not you and you are not him/her. Use the water of support to help his or her shortcomings, and you will be putting water on the fire of domestic violence.

Deprivation

Far too many people living in homes, shelters, walking the streets, locked up in prison, or addicted to substances of some kind are victims of domestic violence. The reason they got this way is because of deprivation of something. If one was to evaluate

33

what really is missing in those lives, the underline answer would be LOVE because love is the under-score needed by every human being. You may buy a Bentley car, build a mansion, save millions of dollars, and travel everywhere as far as the road can take you, but you would still feel an emptiness if you are being deprived of love. When I say love, I don't mean "Baby I love you" or "Love you." I mean the actions of love that touch the deepest senti-ments of the heart that nothing else could touch. The successful family is measured not by materialistic achievements but by love and children who are born and bread into a family of love will reproduce love in their adult lives. But those who never know love live for the most part nothing else but hostility. These hostile adults get into relationships looking for love and sometimes do get it, but don't know how to return it. They therefore find themselves depriving their relationship of the most fundamental ingredient that keeps it together, and when the relationship gets rocky, the making is there for domestic violence of some form.

You may say I can work around this and still keep the relationship crisp. I do not want to discourage you; however, there are some realities in life that we must face and one of them is, "You cannot teach an old dog new tricks if the dog is not willing to learn." After so many energetic trials to give love and not being able to receive it, you will not be very far from a devastating emotional explosion. Please don't fool yourself. This is feelings and passion that you are sharing that you are not getting back in return. Don't you think that one day every blood vessel in you is going to speak very loud? Of course, yes they will, so before that happens, conquer domestic violence by doing the wisest thing, which is, before you begin to expect love , first show love to yourself, so you can give love to others.

If a person is willing to learn how to show love or is trying in their own feverish way to love, you can possibly work with them because they will be careful to avoid hostility and abuse. But if a person determines within themselves that he or she is not going to make any effort to work on being loving or trying to show it, that means that such an individual premeditates to be hostile to and mean spirited to their relationship. No one deserves to be living in such conditions. After prayer, patience, and counseling, are exercised over a period of time, you may have to start looking at the exit door to avoid becoming a victim of domestic violence or becoming the person that commits the crime perhaps in self-defense. A wise nonviolent decision will be a decision that conquers the venom of domestic violence.

Intimidation:

Some populations around the world have not yet shaken themselves from the uncivilized and inferior mentality and values they put upon themselves. As a result, they find themselves feeling very much intimidated whenever they have to interact with someone who they feel is a threat to their self-confidence. By feeling intimidated, they have set the stage for some kind of involvement in domestic violence due to the fact that these same people with low self-esteem are always on the defensive. The involvement can sometimes be an instant reaction or other times a very slowly built one. The response happens because the intimidated party feels like he or she is being crushed by a more powerful force, and the only natural way to exercise power over that crushed feeling is to react violently. Many of these actions are formed in homes of married couples where the wife may be making more money in her job than the husband or where the wife may have a higher level of education than the husband, and so role conflicts then develop in the home. These are typical cases where lack of understanding and adjustment in roles can cause intimidation and set off violence.

These frictions can be avoided once couples know who they are as individuals and what their individual role is in the home. Often times money and education have a tendency of dictating people's role. For instance, in some places where women (the wife) make more money than the husband, she begins to wear the pants by stepping out of her role and treating her husband as though he is her two-year-old child. She would sometimes yell at him in public, snap at him when he is trying to be humorous, and order him around as if he is in prison. In the case of the man, he would also insult his wife in public, give her no room to make any mistakes, and tell her he is the one that is paying for … . These are the evidence of people whose roles are dictated by money and power, and the long-term effect of this is abusive behavior that can result in serious domestic violence cases.

How can the tide be turned to prevent domestic violence in situations like this?

*The first thing that is very important for each and everyone to know is that you are who you are by GOD's making. You must value your self-worth and the pride that you take of yourself. You should never let yourself feel less than someone else because they may have an education and you don't or because they may have a better job and take home more money than you. That's not something to feel intimidated about because you also have something unique that the same person doesn't have. However, whether or not that is so, no person should evaluate their individuality against material success but rather should tell themselves that they are a high-quality component that cannot be bought, borrowed, or sold. So, there is no need to feel intimidated by others. This mental approach will make couples start focusing not on what they have but on the person they are.

*The second thing is that it shouldn't matter who has a better education or who works for more money. The important thing is for everyone to keep their role and not to overstep their boundaries; then if each individual can focus on the main purpose of the union, love and happiness, and not intimidate each other with talents, gifts, and abilities, then the thought of domestic violence will be placed in exile.

Stop Getting Involved So Soon

Many people start new relationships immediately after they end the old one and were not quite ready for new one, so the relationship becomes rocky and dangerous in a short space of time. Because our generation is prone to quick fixes, we therefore need everything instantly. We want to get to where we are going now, not later, we want to make money instantly, we want to buy a home instantly, we want to have a companion instantly. Although with that we say we are taking our time, yet something tells us that we must take our time but have one instantly. I don't know who told us that will work; however, I am sure that it never works, and will never—ever. The fact is, short cuts and instant action do not produce successful results, especially in relationships. They may get you to where you want to go faster, but you will be missing all the experience that you should have learned because you did not take the long road to get there.

Can you imagine what it is like to have a person with an open wound moving around thinking that if the wound doesn't get treated it will heal by itself as they move on in life? It is quite possible for the wound to close but with a high risk of infection. The scenario gives an idea of what it is like to step into a relationship too soon after stepping out of one with deep emotional pain that is without closure. Without a shadow of a doubt, entering a new relationship with a condition like that is really doing nothing else but opening up a door to domestic violence because pain from the previous wound becomes the baggage in a new environment.

As much as a person may feel that they must have a companion at all times in their life, it would not be worth risking life to do so under those unresolved conditions. That is, relationships should begin with both individuals thinking clearly, consciously, and decisively. It should never develop until the past is put away, closure is completed, and a new page is ready to be written on.

The purpose of doing so is healthy for a long loving relationship that has no potential and no appetite for domestic violence. There is no timing on how soon a person should start a relationship after ending one. The advice that I would give is not to rush into it because you may have your eyes or mind on someone and believe that they may get away from you. That will not be whatever plan GOD have for you will never get away from you. It may be that you have to wait for a long time; please just wait because you will enjoy the long wait. Sometimes you may have to also wait long because the one you want to start a new relationship with still have some residue that is very small but still lingering. Entering in a relationship with those residues may also rub off unintentionally on the innocent party and cause conflict to set in the union. This residue could be anything from previous drug addiction to a heavy addiction for sports. You may feel that you can handle these residues because the individuals are no more actively involved in them, but that's a mistake. If you ever have the experience of living with someone who has not been fully cleared from their previous habits, you would find out that the amount of work it takes to live with the un–cleared person can in turn provoke the recovering party to become loaded with very aggressive behavior, and that's not the experience you want. Your aim is to keep such behaviors from your doors. To be able to conquer domestic violence in this capacity is to let pursuers wait for you and you wait for them. If the relationship is going to be, it will be; if it is not, it will not. Somebody's death, sanity, and life will be saved by waiting. Another mistake that everyone should avoid is not to take someone in a relationship and try to clean them up because you want a relationship so desperately. You may have some professional skills in a particular area, but you would not be taken very seriously with what you are doing and respect may be lost for you knowing that there are feelings involved. Your close premature involvement can invite certain expectations, and when there is a disappointment, violent outbursts could be the product. It is necessary to keep the discretionary distance and handle yourself in a respectable and professional manner.

The habit of getting involved in a relationship too soon does have its popularity around the world where there are no restrictions, but consequences are damaging because those who do so have very little respect in their relationships, and wherever respect is lost; abusive cursing, swearing, and name calling take the seat. This is not the kind element that will conquer domestic violence. Therefore, every heated person needs to take their time and wait long enough before getting involved because there are many unknown kinks that need to be straighten out to prevent domestic violence occurrences, and they can be straightened out only with waiting the time out.

Lock A Dollar Up:

One important piece of life that we all sometimes forget is "Nothing in life last forever." The families we live within our home will all one day grow up and decide to go on their own. The new car we have right now will eventually wear out, and we will have to buy another one or do without. The friends we have now may not be the same friends we will have ten or twenty years from now. Some things will change; the job we have now may even change, and when that changes our financial position, both present and future also change. The problem that many of us have is that we are spendthrift individuals; we have very little or no control over what we do with money. We want to buy everything we see, and we don t use everything we buy, but the money is already spent, and we are left short.

We forget to concentrate on the things that we need rather than what we want, and as a result we run ourselves partially broke or just broke. No longer is the rent and paying the mortgage more important than traveling to Las Vegas to put at risk the last few dollars. No longer are the groceries more important than stacking up Coors Light in the corners of the house. I wish that we would stop for a moment and consider what we as a generation are doing with our dollars. I am not by any means implying that we should not have some type of fun in our life—yes we should—but I am sure we can find a better way and a way that will allow us not to be too frivolous with our dollars but to spend some wisely and lock a dollar up carefully for dry days.

By this time some of you reading this book may be asking what does any of this have to do with preventing domestic violence. I am sure we are not strangers to the number of domestic violence recorded down through the years on television and in the newspapers as a result of financial difficulties in the home. I realize that every one of those situations has its own technicalities, but the underlying problem was a dollar that could not be found in times of need.

Here is a fact that's not debatable: "money is not all to life", but money plays a big part of where we live, how we eat, what we wear, how far with education we can go, the quality of care we receive, how economically comfortable we are, and the level of longevity financial stability. These are some of the concerns most people have when they enter into union of marriage. So we see that even if we were trying to deny the importance of money, the fact is, we just cannot live without money. Our generation must learn to lock up a dollar as a habit; that is, save some money somewhere . The reason I emphasize this is because we will all face some days in our lives when the dry days stare us in our face, perhaps because the source of income has been cut off or there are difficult, uncontrollable economic changes, illnesses of some kind, difficult economic expenses, or increases of financial demands to keep the family live stable. When a dollar is put away somewhere, we can always go to where it is and use it to supplement the demands. This extra dollar helps to eliminate some domestic contention in the home among the families that would have happened because of the financial pressure that would have been felt then and also teaches the children of that family how to prepare financially for dry days by the money saving pattern they have seen with their parents.

As the pattern is followed from generation to generation, it will help a large group of people and prevent the unnecessary stress and violence that comes from financial pressure. Once this knowledge of "lock a dollar up" gets moved around in the current and future generation, it will take the sting out of domestic violence motivated by financial pressure, and future generations will be able to have a better hope at least of handling financial pressure in their marriage that has the potential to cause domestic violence.

Thoughts To Ponder:

- Every dollar wasted could be a dollar vested.
- Save the jeopardy by locking up the money.
- The profession you have today may work for today. but the job market require a new need tomorrow.
- "I love you" only will not work with your spouse and the economy—they both need more.
- Planning wisely is a conquering tool that will destroy the thoughts of a fool.

We should never ever underestimate the potential impact that can inflict a family when finances are low and the needs are still the needs but there is not much in store to maintain those needs. Neither should we believe that we are above certain reactions when the crisis is at the door. I agree that everyone will not be bothered by the same crisis, but I do believe that there will be some of you acting out in such way in a financial crisis that could possibly open the door to invite potential domestic violence . I am at this moment writing to you asking you to lock a dollar up to reach back for later and conquer that potential in your family. It may mean that you may have to find the most unpopular way of saving that money; nevertheless the important idea is that domestic violence will not have a chance, at least in this particular area if the cards are played right.

Don't Be Too Quick To Assume:

There are many juries who have never been in a courtroom but have already tried cases, judged defendants in domestic disputes, and sentenced them to misery in their lives. There are also many jealous husbands, wives, husbands-to-be and wives-to-be, children, and other family member who have already assumed what they want to assume and have in their past caused disturbances in and among their families that resulted in domestic violence. Regrettably many mothers, fathers, and children have been previously affected in these ordeals, but these episodes do not have to continue; they can change to eliminate and prevent domestic violence that is caused based on assumptions.

Our world of communication has changed and is constantly improving more than what it was twenty years. Today people are more openly having conversations, socializing, and becoming more comfortable with each other's company in our modern social age. Though it's good on one hand, it can be in some respects be dangerous on the other hand if not moderated, for there are those who cannot handle too much socialization so they make a monster out of social and friendly situations.

It would be naïve to think that some social moments and intentional conversations are not without ulterior motives. Realistically, there are those whose frequent socialization and conversation are with something in the back of the mind, but it is unfair to put everyone in the same boat believing that they are all going into the same direction. Not all of them are; some are just people who have sincere and genuine intentions of keeping the lines of communications open for a platonic relationship and nothing more.

If you are a jealous person who allows your mind to run away with you, you could find yourself in deep trouble if you notice that your spouse is frequently conversing with someone that you have bad feelings about. The first thing that begins to happen with you is that whatever negative perception formed in your mind sends impulses all over your body telling your body to react according to what is being felt. Because of the jealous message that has already settled in the mind, the reaction will of course be nothing but a negative response, which could be anything from verbal abuse to physical harm followed by other abnormal behavior that further increases domestic violence.

I must state that some of these reactions are unnecessary and do not warrant an abusive or violent behavior. What would be really helpful is for the jealous individual to seek some form of help because he or she may be a serial jealous person and not know it. Such a person would get jealous even if a fly were to pass by their spouse. They are constantly jealous, and when there is no reason to be, they find a poor reason.

There shouldn't be any embarrassment to admit that such a person have a problem and need to get help real quick. The quicker they get help, the less likely they are to harm others and themselves. The longer they stay without help, the more vulnerable they become in reacting to what they think they saw and consequently allow graves or prison doors to welcome more victims. I know that pride and piousness could magnify themselves to discourage the idea of getting help for the over jealous behavior that one may have, but it must be noted that pride always precedes destruction, and a pompous and haughty spirit always precedes a fall. To conquer domestic violence because of jealousy would mean that people who are candidates of serial jealousy must overcome their pride, pompousness, and embarrassment and find themselves in a jealousy remediation treatment center or some other professional place of cure.

While the serial jealousy behavior is being worked on, the individuals who may be causing the jealousy also needs to do some work. For instance, if you are a person who knows that you are saddled with an extremely jealous spouse, you should by this time know what would agitate jealousy from what would not and should try to reduce circumstances that would escalate the problem. You should also work along with your spouse to build trust in your relationship so that a sense of security is felt on your spouse's behalf. Don't ignore the problem by saying "get over it"; this will only develop into a bigger and more complex problem if you do so, and since your aim is to conquer any notion of domestic violence in this particular area of life, ignorance will not do. You should, perhaps on a dinner date or some impromptu engagement, have a very detailed conversation with your spouse and assure him or her that you will do all that is within your power to eliminate the unnecessary and do what is necessary. While you are expressing your efforts to change because you want to give your spouse some hope to a better relationship and prevent friction, you should at the same time be clear and decisive to your spouse, that you understand the situation of the serial jealousy that they carry; however, although you are trying to please them to the best of your ability, you cannot walk on pins and needles because doing so may partially resolve the jealous behavior, but you will never feel like yourself walking on pins and needles.

After you have done everything you can to help your spouse including prayer, and nothing has changed, you may have to discuss physical parting for an indefinite period of time to have a better control on preventing domestic violence.

Very often we hear the words "you are the problem." We hear it regularly among couples especially when there is a raging argument. Nevertheless, the raging flames does not put out fights; they only get worse. If those words could change to" let us solve the problem", we would conquer with these words many forms of domestic violence, for it will take the focus off who is to be blamed and put us on our aim.

When a jealous spouse comes to grips with themselves and admits they have a real serial jealousy problem, instead of stalking, checking phone numbers in cell phones, checking wallets for maybe scrap papers, monitoring the activities of their spouses, they will then be able to get help that will equip them to conquer domestic violence rather than getting into deep trouble by their quickness to assume.

Step-Children Should Respect Step-Parents

Due to the high divorce rate and marital separation in America, many children are left without their biological parents in their homes and have to settle for living with their stepmother or stepfather. The changes within them could be devastating for everyone, but more so for the children if not properly transitioned. Therefore, very careful steps must be taken to ensure that there is understanding and education for a smooth transition.

Sometimes adults expects the overnight adjustment from children, and when that does not happen, adults then find themselves in a retaliating zone, damaging the children more than they have already been. Right at this juncture, domestic violence begins like wildfire because the children are rebelling, the stepmother or stepfather is attacking, the biological father or mother is defending, and everyone finds themselves in a war zone, perhaps getting extremely physical with each other.

It is unfair to expect every child in the home to adjust immediately after one of the biological parents has gone from the home. Some of the children will, but there will be always one or two who will find it very difficult to do so, especially if that child or children have a very strong relationship with the departed parent.

Naturally, whoever is left with the children would like to continue on with their life, and as a means of doing so, they enter into a new relationship where they then bring the stepparent into the home to live with the children of a previous marriage. Many stepparents sometimes walk into marriages like this and feel like they have to prove themselves right away, so they begin to throw their weight around by becoming overaggressive to the stepchildren and lose their respect before they even begin to develop a relationship with the children. Consequently, when respect is lost for the head of any home, then chaos is the result in the family. One could take every ideal shortcut to restore lost respect, but it will never happen until the headship is corrected. Ideally, some possible steps to take to prevent and conquer domestic violence with stepchildren and stepparents relationships are:

– Every stepfather should learn to exercise patience and let adjustments come to him rather than overtaking them at the expense of losing touch with your "new family." They must keep in mind that this new family is one that they really don't know much about, so they need to slow down and learn the ropes before they can take charge. The adjustment for you Mr. Stepfather may mean that there will be times when you have to swallow some things that you normally would not have swallowed, but your underlying goal is to establish yourself in your new family and lead them with integrity and pride to a fruitful destiny; therefore, you will have to suffer the pain before you can get to the comforts. Great soldiers are those who accept the bruises of the battle but still remain soldiers, so for you to be able to get to the point of confidently taking your new family to your expected goal, you must withstand the test of rejection and with patience find your way to the place where you convince your stepchildren that you love them and are interested in their affairs of life. By doing so, you will not be found around the table pleading for respect; instead, you will earn it, but only if you take your time.

While this method does work most of the time, other times, Mr. Stepfather, you may need to communicate some things through the mother to the children when the need is. The method of approach here helps the children to give respect to you for when the mother say to the children your stepfather suggested that ..., automatically the children get the sense that their mother looks up to and respects their stepfather; therefore, they too begin to feel the obligation of respecting their stepfather. With time, a bond will soon develop, and what had all the ingredients to be turned into a domestic violent environment will no longer be, but with patience and skill, stepfathers can get respect from step children and develop a bond of peace and unity.

– Stepmothers sometimes need to take the very same actions as stepfathers. Do not take too many passive actions on the stepchildren before you are able to have a relationship with them. Yes, it may be a little easier with you to get into their lives than a stepfather can, especially if they are young men. However, remember if you move too fast, you can be rejected and disrespected faster. The residence of stepchildren and stepparents in a home offers a strong challenge, which can turn into a war zone or arena if all the members of the family are unwilling to make adjustments, but when adjustment is made, the bond and union can be so powerful that domestic violence in that family will become a foreign language. There is absolutely no doubt that stepchildren should respect their step parents. However, for that to take place, stepparents must discipline themselves to earn it and not to demand it. They must also show respect to their stepchildren and avoid provoking them to anger. Everyone must treat each other the way they would like to be treated.

Chapter II

An Honest Amnesty Program

America for many centuries has been the country where many people from all walks of life come to pursue a better life, a better education and for some, freedom from other burdens that have been placed upon them in their native country. Because of the different nationalities that are living in America, we can almost say that the whole world lives in America and if not the whole, ninety nine percent of the whole world. That is, it is an international country.

I wish that it could be said that the whole world or the ninety nine percent of the whole world that lives in America were all legal residence or citizens of America. Unfortunately, it cannot be said for a noticeable percentage of the residents that live in America are not legal immigrants. Among this percentage of illegal immigrants, domestic violence is not reported, so women, especially unmarried and living in homes with boyfriends, are victimized by the violence and the children of those women have to watch the violent abusive behavior done to their moms. In recent years even to present, elected official and Congress have battled with several bills submitted that would give illegal aliens limited legal status in America, but none of the several attempts has become successful so far. Meanwhile the illegal population is growing, the domestic violence among that group is silently increasing, and the teachers in the different classroom are trying to find a solution to the little children who are acting out in class because of the trauma they are experiencing constantly at home as a result of the violence. Under the illegal status position, domestic violence will never be fully conquered because victims are not coming forward to report the violence for fear of deportation, so the violent crime then has the potential to move quickly to another generation, which is the children who, having seen it in their early life, will then practice it later as they grow up to become teenagers and adults . With regard to the illegal circumstances also, the statistics of the government report in reference to domestic violence will never be correct for only the reported violence are recorded, and the many unreported acts of violence within the illegal alien group is without number but at the same time too frequent.

Just to be able to stay in America many women are willing to risk their lives with the violence, hoping that just the idea of living under the bright lights of America will soften the pain as they await another abusive moment by the monster they live with. If they could find an alternative that could ease the pain, they would more than welcome the idea. I suggest that they bring an end to the pain at whatever cost for there is no worse feeling than the feeling of pain.

What should be understood is that the unrecorded domestic violence right now is conquering an undocumented community, and police officers and other forms of help cannot be of service to these victims because the cases are unreported. This form of violence is taking over the victims' children's' lives as it hits society in its fullest force. Having an honest amnesty program in America and elsewhere would allow:

– Hidden domestic violence victims to report to the police on the cause, the extent of the violence, and the motive. This type of information is necessary for proactive purposes as a means of conquering violence. This action may also help by securing the affected parents and children involved and placing them into a safe place of recovery from their long abusive violent environment.

– An honest amnesty program will allow HIDDEN victims and potential victims of domestic violence to attend various workshops and other educational programs where they will learn how to handle active and potential domestic violence and the other different helps that are available. Whenever victims of any type of crime use the resources that are available to them, the strength of the crime is weakened, and the statistics of the crime then drop because the weapons to fight are in action.

– With an honest amnesty program more of the women who are illegal will now be able to apply for jobs and work to hold their own money, do their own shopping without having to wait on the yelling and abusive treatment from a man before they can get twenty dollars to take care of themselves. Of the money worked for by these ladies, tax will be taken out, and the taxes will help the government to provide and fund more educational programs to conquer domestic violence.

Obviously it sounds good to read the lowing statistical rate of domestic violence or any other crime from a piece of paper, but what good are the statistics to anyone if the real truth is not revealed. The real truth is, there are many people in hiding with the violence, and unless there is a trustworthy program or some other incentive given to bring them out of the hiding places and report their domestic violence encounters, an underground operation will still be going on, and the figures will not be accurate, and society will reproduce its kind as violent behaviors gets out of hand. This is why an honest amnesty program is needed so that all the violence is reported and full measures can be taken against this violence.

When most people hear of an amnesty program, the first thing that comes to mind is getting legal status. It is true that you may have legal status, but technically it goes a little further than that; it helps to protect people from becoming victims of domestic violence by saving them entering into premature marital relationship as some type of business deal that has all the signs of violence. Many of the people who were pressured to marry in the past to secure legal status in the specific country of residence at that time have now divorced but have gone through many encounters of domestic abuse and violent behaviors before they do so. With an amnesty program, there wouldn't be any pressure to marry just to have legal status; therefore, the chances of marrying to the wrong person are slim, and when such is the case, contention and aggressive behaviors that lead to domestic violence are diminished.

The aim of conquering domestic violence especially among illegal aliens can be better done with a credible trustworthy honest amnesty program that will remove the fear of deportation in the hearts of hiding domestically abused women.

Testimonies

These are the testimonies of some victims of domestic violence. The victims would like to remain anonymous, therefore John Doe and Jane Doe are used for names.

Testimony By Jane Doe:

I was born in one of the countries of Central America and immigrated to America at the age of ten. I am a very sociable and outgoing person but when I met my ex-husband, I became very dedicated to him and to my marriage so I narrowed down my social life just for him because I loved him and I wanted us to make it together in life. I was always the traditional kind of person who believes in raising a close knit family so I made every effort to do the best that I can to please my husband. I loved my husband dearly, but I was so much in love with him that I could not see how much he was abusing me. Sometimes he yells at me for no reason, he called me all names. He tells me I am no good, he tells me I am not sharp, meaning I am illiterate and many other forms of mental abuse he would do to me. However with the all the name calling I still hung in the marriage hoping that something will get better. There were times when he would leave the home without telling me where he is going and I would sit around and wait for a call but did not get one until many days later. Not only was I verbally and mentally abused but I was also physically abused. There were some days when the abuse was just mental and verbal and there were other times when it was mental, verbal and physical. I cried for many days, and nights trying to bring an immediate end to the pain I felt but matters only got worse. I question myself and wish to die in the process. Nothing in my life meant anything to me anymore, I became depressed, lost my self-esteem, lost my desire for my husband and even lost my motivation to take care of myself as a woman. Money and things meant nothing to me then all I wanted was to free myself of this horrible domestic abuse. My pain was more than I can bear, but through it all whenever I am in public I had to front things with a smile that was not real. Physically my whole body went in trauma for many years and I lost weight as well as some of the hair on my head that I cherished so much. I felt like I was just existing without a purpose in life., but my faith in GOD was strong enough to make me believe that someday GOD would deliver me once and for all from the abuse I suffered as a woman and as a wife. I kept praying to GOD and one day my husband decided that he was going to move to another state away from me. That he did and in the process of time we then got divorced. I was still sad for a while until one day I came to grips with myself and decided to rise up out of my dilemma. When I did that I was not alone for I was able to do so with the strong support of my brother and support of an elderly gentleman. They both showed me love and care in a very respectable way and led me back to the road of life where I found true meaning and excitement in life again.

As I look back on my life and the unfortunate situation of domestic abuse, I realized that I never wanted to live that life but I settle for it with my husband because I was a product of domestic violence in my younger life when I had to constantly see my step father beating up my mother.

I also realized that had it not been for the support that I got to help, strengthen me emotionally, I would probably be a wreck today.

My message to all who may find themselves in domestically abusive situations is to:

a) Pray to GOD for help
b) Make a decision to get out and start doing something right a way
c) Get support from families, friends or some type of agency that will help.

If you can do these three things you will have some tools in your hands to conquer domestic violence.

Testimony Of John Doe:

I am fifty years old; I was married to my ex-wife for fourteen years. I did not have any children with my ex-wife because she already had four children who were not my biological children, but I embraced them as though they were my own children. I loved my ex-wife but I never believe that she loved me because she was always screaming at me. When I look at her she snapped at me asking me why I am looking at her. Whenever I leave for work and try to kiss her good bye, she wipes her face and sometimes pushes me away. When I walk in the house she says that I am walking too loud and call me insulting names, when I try to walk soft she tells me to walk like a man in the house. I could not correct the children at any time or she would tell me they are not my children I should mind my business. I could not come to any common ground with her, I couldn't do anything right, couldn't say anything right, I could not even wear anything right.

She was always cursing me for anything even if I had nothing to do with it. Sometimes right after our deepest intimate moments she would curse me and call me the worse of names you can think of. I was never happy, I felt depressed all the time because the abuse was slowly but surely eating away on my manhood. As a man my self-esteem dropped very low, I was very frustrated and did not want to be in the company of other men because I did not feel like one. Many times when I get into my car to go to work I asked myself the question of why I should really work. One day we were both going to the super market and on our way I stopped the car suddenly to avoid an accident and she call me a big stupid dummy. Often times I contemplated to walk away from the marriage because I felt very sick of the mental and verbal abuse. I didn't have any drive to talk to my mother or my sister, for it seem as though this abuse shut me down from females even my own female family members.

Eventually one day I took the courage to say to my ex-wife that I had enough of the abuse and I was going to leave. When I was hoping for her to be sorrowful or say nothing, instead she said that I was doing her a favor by leaving because she never really loved me, anyway, she only married me just to have a male figure in the home but it's not needed anymore.

Tears then came to my eyes and I broke down emotionally because I realized I wasted fourteen years of my life.

It was difficult for me to find myself immediately because I felt like I experienced a punch in the head and the stomach at the same time when I told her I had enough.

For many months I stayed depressed until an old friend came to see me at my apartment in the basement of a house. He knocked the door several times before I could come to the door .When I let him in he was so glad to see that after sharing some of his divorce experience with me he helped me clean up my dirty apartment and promise he would visit me more frequently. I welcomed his visit and noticed I was beginning to put my past behind my back and rise to a new level in life. My emotional strength was renewed, my dreams were revived, my hope was rebuilt again and I started trusting in myself to feel that life is not over. As time passed I was back on my feet living a normal civil life. I always say thanks to my friend for the strong support he game me just when I needed it.

I would not mind telling the world that supporting friends in domestic abuse situations are more valuable than gold put into your hands.

Form A Supporting Cast

Even though we may all feel that we are indepen-dent and don't need the help of others, that is not so. Perhaps in a punitive way we do, for we don't want others inflicting pain on us, but in a general social sense we do need the helping hand of others. Most ships in the ocean are not by themselves; they have other vessels with them known as life boats that are activated in cases of emergencies where crew and passengers' lives are at risk. Apart from the lifeboats there are other coast guards ships that are constantly on the watch for any disaster at sea that could endanger lives. If the captain of a ship knows that while sailing he would be without lifeboats or that assistance of coast guards, maybe he would think twice about sailing, especially if the journey was going to be a long one. Realistically nothing functions properly by itself, and anything that seems to be working by itself has technical support of something else that is not visible. Domestic violence — verbal, mental, and physical — has been in the light for a very long time but had too many loopholes that made it difficult to conquer.

Many marriages today need to plug up the loophole of non-support and replace it with a supporting cast. This means newlyweds should give themselves some type of flexibility to learn from the veterans of successful marriages some ideas, thoughts, skills of how to keep their marriage fresh and interesting to prevent uncalled-for problems. We must take into consideration that no one is marrying a perfect well-put-together individual; everyone has some type of weakness or imperfection that they are bringing into a marriage . Someone's imperfection could be not knowing how to spend, another could be not being able to cook a nutritious meal, another could be not being able to communicate clearly. All these are handicaps that can take a marriage of good intentions and turn it into violent modes and bitter endings. This does not have to be if everyone will admit they have imperfections, acknowledge them, and allow some support from genuine, sincere, and respectable mentors of successful marriage to help in the areas of weakness .Although this may seem a little uncomfortable, it is really nothing to hang your head down about; instead, it is more beneficial for the marriage for holes that need plugging in terms of support, and naturally it is better to plug a fault in a relationship with the support of others than to leave it open to become a monstrous experience. In truth and in fact, there are many different helps and support of mentors that are available today to relationships for the conquering of domestic violence, and they should be used, for when they are used, they will reduce the high statistics level of domestic violence.

I am aware that our society is very private and sensitive; therefore, some will never reach out to take advantage of the available help in the name of "I don't want anyone to know my business because I don't know their business." Let me be clear in saying that I am not inviting you to make your life a federal case or a public announcement; however, you must ask yourself this question. Is it better for me to bury my pride and get some support to plug a small deficiency in my relationship that can seal off any potential for domestic violence, or should I just leave it open because I don't want anyone to know my business and allow it to become a disaster? If you are a smart person, you would rather ten people know what you are working on or getting support for to keep domestic violence away than to allow ten thousand people to learn about you in the newspapers and on television. You should take advantage of all necessary supporting cast immediately, for they will strengthen your relationship so that you can in turn strengthen someone else's relationship and become their supporting cast .

There are many forms of a supporting cast that people used to uphold a relationship when it is already broken, but the point that I would like our readers to hold is not to wait for a relationship to be broken and on the verge of becoming domestically violent to apply the supporting cast. You should fix the little kinks that have the ability to be dangerous and put the plug of a supporting cast on the agitated wound that could flare up. Domestic violence is better conquered when actions taken are proactive rather than reactive.

These are some questions and concern that people in relationships deal with on a daily basis. In these situations, whether it is for better or for worse, they were able to make decisions. Some might have regrets of poor decision making; others might be very happy over a good decision. Although one person may not make their decision the same as the other, the outcome of every decision must be that it conquers domestic violence whether it's by prevention, confrontation, caution, or conviction.

Decision Making Exercise

You have been married to the same man for 32 years. He was married before, you weren't. You just recently learned that in his previous marriage he was very abusive to his wife and now after thirty-two years you notice that he is getting to be abusive to you. Both of you are senior citizens about 65 years old. How are you going to conquer this violence by stopping it?

Here are some thoughts that come to mind:

- I am too old to put up with this
- I am too old to start over again
- I don't want the police to get involved
- I just ignore him, he will stop some day
- He is just getting old and miserable.

All these thoughts may be legitimate; however, what you are faced with is domestic violence inflicted upon you. Your thoughts should be not to work around it but to tell yourself that you are going to take measures to conquer it, even if the measure is not popular at your age.

You are constantly threatened and yelled upon by the man who says he will love you until death parts both of you. In spite of what he said you constantly call the police for the violent domestic action. Whenever the police show up at your door, you tell the cops that everything is ok; he was just playing, but he stopped.

Deep in your heart you know very well that you are dealing with domestic violence, but you want to sugarcoat the actions, thinking that if you do, that you will appease the situation, and it will go away. If you choose to accept it or not, the actions are what they are—domestic violence—and sugarcoating those actions is not conquering them.

You are in a marital relationship with a woman (your wife) who has a medical condition that requires medication. Whenever she does not take her medication she becomes abusive to you. She calls you insulting names in public; she continually shouts at you to the point where you are afraid to be in public with her. You tell yourself that she will be ok as long as she gets her medication, but she refuses to take her medication, and in the meantime the violent actions step up and knock.

You don't want to call any professional help, for if you do you are afraid she might be pulled away from you temporarily, so you accept the abuse and try to live but live in grief. Is that conquering domestic violence?

You marry someone who does not care to have any acknowledgement of your family. He or she tries very hard to isolate you from your family and told you if you don't stop going by their house or stay off the phone, you will pay the price. You love your family anyway, so you cannot isolate yourself from them. At the same time you love your husband or wife and would not want to lose your marriage, so what you did was not to isolate yourself or stop talking to them, so you communicate with them secretly when your spouse is not around to see. I sure don't mind telling you that you will not be conquering domestic violence then; instead, it is conquering you.

It's quite possible that one or more of these examples pertains to some of you reading this book. The frustration that you feel is now telling you that the relationship you now have is the worst decision that you have ever made in your life. If that is so, you should be grateful that you have come this far in life and through the experience you recognize that a change is needed, and for that to happen, you will need a supporting cast of some kind to lift you above any unforeseen action of domestic violence.

Extinguish The Silence:

As good as silence is, it can become a detriment depending on the circumstances and the type of silence. For example if there is a verbal dispute in motion and a person chooses to stay quiet to avoid agitation or argument, that form of silence may be considered a silence of wisdom. If the individual is silent because he or she is just naturally a quiet person and does not talk too often but is yet cheerful and pleasant quite naturally this really would not become a concern to anyone for the nature of the silences is harmless.

When a person, on the other hand, who is not known to be quiet by nature chooses to stay silent in a vindictive manner with a motive to be destructive, that type of silence is very dangerous and raises a red flag. With domestic violence there is no one way of becoming violent; instead, there are several ways, but all the different routes that are being used lead only to one action and that is a violent action. If all the channels that lead to this one action were to be brought under control, the action would become powerless, and the fight against domestic violence would not need any attention, for its bite would be ineffective. We do wish that this was the case today, but realistically, it's not. We are now faced with a silent generation that makes it difficult to control evil premeditative actions, and that type of behavior is one of the major reasons why domestic violence has escalated to where it is today.

When you have relationships where the individuals involved are passing each other in the home and are not speaking, you must know that perhaps not immediately, but somewhere in the future, there will be disaster. When you have relationships where everything that needs to be told to the mother or father is through one of the children by the husband or wife saying "tell your mother ..." or "tell your father ...,"that relationship is either already experiencing domestic violence or about to do so.

When you have a relationship where husband, wife, children, all communicate to each other by body language, you should know that the active teeth of domestic violence is present. It is easy to say "I did not say a word" to cause a problem; that may be so that you never said a word; nevertheless, the actions you show speak louder than words, and if they are provocative actions, they are enough to light the fire of domestic violence. Because we human beings are creatures of verbal communications, we are expected to communicate verbally, if not all the time then most of the time, and when that is lacking, especially in a relationship, someone in the process is momentarily experiencing domestic abuse and may later take it to a very physical level with confrontation. Sometimes it may lead to another form of domestic violence where one of the individuals decides that the way to relieve themselves of all the stress and pain that they are experiencing is to take their own life. It really doesn't matter what form of domestic violence results from silent communication; what really matters is that it is a channel that leads to the violence, and everyone must take every step to conquer it, either through prevention or cure by communicating clearly and respectfully to each other.

Some Ways To Extinguish Silence

If there is an ongoing breakdown of communication in your relationship that is now resorting to silence between the two parties, remember that a relationship is only as good as you make it. Meaning, what you settle for is what it will be. Everyone should not sit in the environment and blame the other for breakdown; someone should rise above the circumstance, put away their pride and finger pointing, then take the initiative to begin some type of conversation to break the silence. This action should not belittle you since your aim is to conquer domestic violence. You may find it difficult at first to take charge of such situations as well as not getting much cooperation from the other individual(s) involved. In any event you must continue to press for what you are trying to accomplish. If after a while you feel as though you are not getting the success that you want, take a step further and have an informal conversation with a group around your silent partner and allow some humorous moments for him or her to laugh. In those moments mention a few funny things about yourself and a few serious things as well, take some responsibilities of some areas in life where you made some bad decisions in life, and compliment your silent partner for enduring with you through it all.

Doing so you will soon find out that what you have done is to put a crack into that sediment of silence, for slowly but surely your silent partner soon begins to open up by having an occasional conversation with you. Be cautious not to be too eager for a quick flow of conversation, but accept it as it comes and build up the conversation until you get it to what it should be. By doing so you would have administered a lethal dosage of medication into the teeth of domestic violence. I do not promise you an easy journey, but I can tell you that the fight is worth it, for you might have saved the health and lives of many, including yours, since silent actions can be very devastating and fatal.

If there is no breakdown in communication in your relationship don't count yourself above it;, it can happen to you since time changes, and human beings also change with time. Take all necessary precautions to preserve the good communication that you have going now, for it only takes a second to start the downhill journey of silence. Keep your conversation in your relationship mixed—that is, make it funny, exciting, interesting, flavoured—and when it's time to talk about business, give it your utmost attention with all wisdom. Never try to be sarcastic or ironic unless it's a humorous moment and even when that is the moment, limit the irony and sarcasm for they can touch very sensitive areas of one's life.

Don't wait for any one person to start the flow of conversation, for its each person's duty to communicate to the other. When there is open communication, there will be clear understanding and very little chance to entertain resentments and evil thoughts, which are two of the main ingredients of domestic violence.

Silence at times has its place and can be deemed necessary to maintain some sanity, but on the other hand, silence can be used in a relationship as a weapon of domestic violence when it is out of control.

To conquer domestic violence in the area of silent communication, is for every couple or family to make sure that the evil force of silent communication becomes disrupted, and if for any reason there must be a silent communication, it must be short-lived, positive, constructive, and fruitful; anything else other than those qualities must be trashed and considered as devices that establish domestic violence.

Education At All Channels

There will always be some people who are not strangers to domestic violence. They are either the victim of the violence or they are the ones who instigate the violence. Some of these people grew up in violence and don't know any better than to do what they have seen around them for a long time. The way they resolve issues is by slapping, punching, and kicking, and the way they communicate is by yelling at the top of their voices. Are these people hard to live with? Absolutely, yes, but at the same time, not all domestic abusers are of the same nature. Some of them could want to learn how to conquer domestic violence, but they don't know where to start; others believe that if you leave it alone, one day it will just go away, which of course is not the way it works.

We are very much aware that domestic violence is not subject to any particular class of people; it introduces itself to any class, anywhere at any given time, and spreads quickly if not controlled.

Knowing that domestic violence is like a snake that shows up unannounced, it would be a good idea to conquer the potential of it by implementing some domestic violence education into some channels where a large volume of the population flows. For example, the motor vehicle registry department: it is through this agency that everyone passes through to get a driver's license, vehicle registration, and other legal documents that qualify them to operate a vehicle on the road. Some of the applicants passing through the registry have never been exposed to any domestic violence and never believe they will be, but because this monster has the potential to show up anytime at any place among any class, it would be beneficial to be equipped with some type of training during the licensing in case the monster shows up in your house.

For the people that have been and are still in some form exposed to it, a training through the registry of motor vehicles might be the only way to get them to understand and deal with domestic violence to defeat it. Having training as a part of procedures to obtain a license and registration would not only bring a stronger awareness, a greater exposure to prevention and cure, but would help to bring respect on an individual level.

Another avenue where domestic violence training could be implemented is through some of the subsidy programs that are available in many cities and countries. This is not to say that people on subsidy of whatever kind are the ones most likely to suffer domestic violence. They are not more likely than anyone else, but wherever there is an opportunity plug a hole before a rat gets into it and does damage, it should be done.

Many people applying for subsidy houses do so because they want to be able to put their lives back together and live an affordable and manageable life where they could properly take care of themselves and their families. It is very unfortunate that some of the applicants that qualify for the subsidies after assuring the property managers that the names on the lease are the ones that will be the tenants, then later on sneak in other parties to live in the apartments, unknown to the landlord or property manager.

The concern here is not whether or not someone has the right to do what they have done, or because a person is paying their own bill so they can do what they choose to do. The concern is these are some of the potential avenues for domestic violence, and a sense of awareness should be made known.

You may ask how this could be a potential avenue for domestic violence.

One should never be naïve about people who want no responsibility. Such people have nothing to lose and because they know that, they are not afraid to take good things and make them bad, destroy things, maintain an irresponsible life style that disrupts your life style because their name is not on a single document in your apartment. In other words they have no responsibility to the property manager or the land lord, so they live a "don't care" life. This type of behavior speaks nothing else but an obvious clash that results in domestic violence.

I am of the firm belief that when legal tenants who find themselves deceived into taking in other tenants into their apartments, they are not thinking of the domestic violence that it would breed; instead they are probably thinking of companionship, comfort, or perhaps helping out someone. However, there is always the notion of deception that escapes our mind but gets captured by someone else who would make sure that it gets into our mind.

Therefore, having domestic violence training as a part of the application and approval process for subsidy housing would be one way of conquering domestic violence, for it will bring to mind the violent potentials of sneaky intruders and would hopefully raise the consciousness of legitimate tenants to keep the intruders out to avoid domestic abuse.

The idea of training and education in these avenues should never be implemented to penalize anyone from having access and privileges, but cities, states, and countries that are attempting to conquer domestic violence should utilize these avenues because a good percentage of every city population flows through these avenues.

Chapter III

Practicing Independence

How fascinating it is to watch the ant in the summer time foraging, making several errands to her nest, carrying food to store up for the long winter months that are ahead of her. I am pretty sure it's hard work for that ant, but in the long run it pays off because she is able to sustain herself and her family through the cold winter. That ant does not want to depend on any other insect other than her kind for food in the winter, so she makes sure that she stores for herself and the rest of the colony for the possibility of any other insect delivering food to her nest could be consequential.

If we were to take a page from the ant's domestic sense, it might help to conquer some areas of domestic violence. Occasionally you may find two ants carrying food to their storage—they might be the married couple—but other times you will find one ant doing it all by herself or himself, showing a sense of independence- that might be the single mother or father, who knows.

The attitude of dependency is not limited to women but also men. The needs may be different, but the idea is the same and that is, depending on someone to do for you because you told yourself that you cannot do it by yourself or you just cannot do it at all.

Right at this point you are preparing the grounds to become a victim of domestic violence through parasitic mentalities because when you become too dependent on someone for your needs and the person is aware that your sole dependence is on him or her, that person could find an opportunity to use you and abuse you until you lose your self-worth and feel extremely useless. If one was to dig deep into the core of many domestically violent relationships, it would not be surprising to find that someone is fully dependent on the other for something; that could be monetary support, emotional support, shelter, companionship, or security of different kinds. Many of these dependencies also do not complain about their violent situations because if they do they would lose their source and would become paralyzed in life because they are afraid to be independent, so they stay and suffer the violence even if it's costing them their good health

There is absolutely no way that any human being should live like that, because not even animals do, and those who are right now living that life should consider taking immediate actions to get out. Stop depriving yourself of a real right to life by telling yourself that you have to depend on him or her for those things so you can't move from where you are, even when it's domestically violent for you. That type of mentality keeps you dependent to take more abuse and not to make you independent so that you can find a new life and become a testimony of achievement to others. The real truth is the attitude you take about yourself. If you tell yourself that you have to depend on someone else to live, then of course that's what you will do every day. If you say to yourself that you will begin to live an independent life, then you will rise up and make the start. Why settle for being treated harshly and violently abused when you can do better than that. The decision to be better and have a better future is all in your hands, so get started and conquer the monster—domestic violence—by making use of the little that is left within you.

This page speaks directly to some of you. You may not have a great education now, but you will get there eventually. You may not have any money anywhere in any bank, but you will get there in time. You may think now it is impossible for you to ever own a home, but do not write yourself off. Many people have been in worse predicaments than you, and they were able to accomplish what looks impossible, and if they can, you can too. Please stand up and stir up the skills that you have buried inside of you: you know, you may be a good cook, a good mother or father, have outstanding domestic skills, or are very good with your hands. Whatever you know that you are good at, put it to work. Don't be concerned about not getting popular; as long as you remain consistent, your work will speak for you, and you could be in demand. However, do your best to exercise your abilities and skills to work wisely, respectfully, and sincerely to be your best in whatever you do so that you do not have to sit around and depend on anyone to use you and violently abuse you because they give you the things of life that you don't have. Do not get excited when you read this page, then forget about everything you plan to do later; you will not be conquering domestic violence. Instead make the first step to start becoming independent in your mind, and then follow it through with actions. You will surprise yourself with the powerful tools that you had been sitting on for many years that could have given you a better opportunity in life before but you never utilized because you became dependent and got stuck in a domestically violent relationship. Now that your eyes are more open, start the conquering process now. Your decision in turn will trickle down to all the generations that follow ,and the conquering message will ring the bells of independence in these generations.

Stopping Compulsary Relationship Disorder

We all make choices on a daily basis to do the things that we want to do. Some of those choices are given long hard and careful thoughts and, with time, are made, while other are made at the snap of the finger. Some of the choices we make take us away from things that we have been acquainted with for a very long time and have become a part of our daily lives but now have completely diminished in our minds because we have removed ourselves from them. Some of the reasons why we do so are because we want change. In some respects we wish we could hold on to those long-acquainted things, but holding on jeopardizes our sanity, so we choose to let go of them and let go without wavering in the process.

Not at all should we be surprised at some of the domestic violence that is caused by compulsory relationship disorders. This behavior is responsible for a great number of domestic violence events, especially among the younger generation. It's time that men and women take a decisive stand on what they want to do next when a relationship ends. I don't mean to close the doors on reconciliation; neither am I saying to be mean, hostile, and inconsiderate. What I am saying is that often times when a relationship ends, one of the parties usually moves out of the home but still wants to have the same relationship as if he or she was still living there. Can you have your cake and still eat it? I am afraid not. If you were driving somewhere where you come to a light and find the light to be green, amber, and red at the same time, you would be confused and not know whether to proceed or to stop; you are at that very moment being subject to danger. That's exactly how some domestic violence occurs: people who break up their relationship one month come back to live together a few months later, then repeat their behavior a few months later and may continue to do so for a long period of time. Needless to say, these in and out relationships are not without promises made that never come to pass. Such actions do nothing else more than agitate, aggravate, and irritate the core of individual sentiments, thus causing them to result in domestic violence.

If you really want to conquer domestic violence in this realm, you should never allow yourself to be beaten with the stick of unfulfilled promises that will come to you with a sweet song. When a relationship ends, you must come to grips with yourself and understand that the relationship ended and not allow the other party the liberty of bouncing like a ball in and out of your life fulfilling their needs and getting their gratification in the name of " you are the only one I love ,I am going to change. " If they were serious about having a loving relationship with you, they would weather out all the storms of life and stick with you, hoping to have better days, but they did not; instead, they chose to leave because they didn't want to change. Under no conditions should you make such a person think that they could live two places at the same time or that your home is their hospital bed. You must let such a person know that they are either going to be here or there, a right turns or a left turn; there should be no medium, for medium in relationship breeds frustration, which further breeds domestic violence.

There are those who were once married couples and have now severed the relationship with each other who will say. "Oh! We are not together anymore; we are just friends, and we meet with each other still anyway." You may play this game for long time, but little do you know you are playing with fire. You need to fix it or completely break it for you cannot prevent domestic violence by sleeping with the lion that you put away.

I know that this is a very harsh advice, but in order to prevent domestic violence, a stand must be taken, and compulsive relationship disorders must be stopped by people who are encouraging them.

Don't Be Carried Away By:

– Your ex stopping at your home saying, "I was just passing through and decide to stop to see how you are doing. Here is fifty dollars to help you through." I wouldn't advise you to take it, especially since you have been doing without it for a long time. Those fifty dollars are to purchase comfort.

– By your ex boasting about what he or she has accomplished since you last saw each other. That may be a bait to get you to be jealous and express your regrets for the departure of you both.

– By your ex's invitation to you to call when you need help with anything. It could be a trap to get very familiar.

– By your ex giving you the car to drive whenever you need. It could be for you to spend several nights where he or she lives.

– By your ex complaining about not being able to have a good meal and sleep in a clean home for a long time. It could be a scheme designed for you to start cooking dinner for him or her to come to your house and spend long hours and get cozy but not to stay.

In conquering domestic violence, one must always be on the lookout for some of these things among exes, because they are very common things that have in the past put past relationships back together for a temporary moment and once the moment is past the relationship keels over again, and violence becomes an issue, because someone was expecting what cannot be given by the other. Evidently, to conquer domestic violence there should always be a steadfast attitude in what you know that you don't want and focus on the better things of life rather than a man or a woman who does not know whether they are going or coming with their own life.

Some Tips To Help

A Code Word Helps

Many people today who are victims of domestic violence could have escaped some of the abuse if they only had someone to help them at the time when the initial abuse started. Not all abusers operate the same way; there are some abusers who will react to what they feel on the spot at any time and are not concerned about who sees them and who hears what they say, and there is another set of abusers who wait for an appointed time when their partner is away from everyone to start their plan of abuse. This type of abuse is the most dangerous because the abused victim could have a difficult time getting anyone's attention for help at their abused moments.

I am not implying that abusive moments takes place only when other people are not around; it would be naïve to think so because many of the victims of domestic violence do suffer abuse even in the presence of their own children. However, in spite of this, it is better for someone else to have an awareness of what is domestically happening with you than to stay silent and suffer abuse. Therefore, if you find yourself living with an abusive mate a few yards away from your neighbor, you should make sure your neighbor is knowledgeable of your situation and give your neighbor a code word that means *help*. Whenever you have accurate suspicion that violent or abusive actions are about to take place, find an effective way to shout out your code word to prevent the violence or abuse .your neighbor then will be aware that you are in trouble and help you by activating the necessary help needed then.

Prep The Car For Takeoff

Some of you have been coached by others who think that they know your domestically violent environment better than you—to fight back your opponent. This may sound good in your ears to do but is not necessarily the best response for you because the situation may get worse, and your abusers already have the upper hand on you, being in a rage. You may be the victim today but you can be a conqueror tomorrow.

If you find yourself in conflict with your abuser, do not take anything for granted, especially if you know the abusive history of that person. Always have your vehicle parked properly; that is, cleared of any obstruction, with enough gas in the tank and have the keys for the vehicle as accessible to you as you possibly can.

Whenever you sense a moment that an abusive or violent behavior is about to happen, discretely move to your vehicle; with all wisdom, get in the car for takeoff mode. Do not return until you have the proper forces and personnel to conquer this violence.

If the home has only one vehicle, you may not have much control over the parking and the gas that is currently in the parked vehicle, but find a way to have access to one of the keys to start the car and use all wisdom to escape.

Keep Phone Numbers Elsewhere

One of the first things abusers do when they are in attack mode is to make sure they destroy the means of communication from the home to the outside world . Some may rip the phones out of the walls, destroy the computers, smash the cell phones, including the victim's cell phone, and even close the windows and doors so that no communication gets outside the house.

I am aware that in today's technological world most people store phone numbers in their cell phones to making calling much easier for them. The technology is great, but if the phone gets destroyed and you do not have any other means of accessing important numbers, it means that you could find yourself in much trouble and may have caused your own dilemma by relying too much on technology.

It would be very beneficial, especially in potential domestic violence situation to store as many phone numbers as you can in your head. If, in a domestic abusive situation, your cell phone is smashed by your abuser, you may have a chance to use your neighbor's phone and call the important numbers you need because you have them at a place that was never smashed or seen.

Get Information

No one should ever live an uninformed life in their surroundings. The place you occupy as your neighborhood is your territory, and you should therefore know what is going on in your territory. Your other neighbors may want to believe that you are the nosy type, but you should never take offence to that; you are only making sure that you get all the information that is necessary for you as a concerned citizen.

In your inquiry, you may learn of scheduled domestic violence meetings and workshops that will be taking place in your neighborhood. Do not pay light attention to it just because you are not in a domestically violent relationship; make every effort to attend the meetings and workshops and also refer the information to as many as you can find in your neighborhood. The idea is that whatever does not affect you now can affect you later, and because we are each other's keeper, you may help to enlighten the minds of other by sharing what you know about domestic violence. The fact is, some people are not informed about how they can conquer domestic violence; that's because they are looking too far away to receive information, while information is right in their neighborhood.

If you fail to keep informed, you may only invite yourself into a trap that you will find out later, for sometimes that person that you fall in love with two houses down from yours that, just moved into your neighborhood and told you they just moved from California is the person who just got out of prison and is on parole serving time for domestic abuse. You may not get everything you want to know, but you sure will get some information that will help you and your children to conquer domestic violence in its early stage.

Guard Your Heart

Whether you are a single person or a married couple, you could become a candidate domestic violence either by being victimized or a perpetrator if you do not guard your heart.

Many involved in domestically violent relationships today are dealing with the question, "How did I get into such relationship?" and of course they are blaming others and situations as the reason for their upside-down relationship .It is only fair to say no one else or nothing else is to be blamed, but the people who make the decision; they did not guard their heart well enough; they messed up.

Though I can name many areas in relationships where people's heart were left unguarded, one of the most dangerous area is infatuation. Infatuation has been destroying relationships on a normal scale for many years, but over a period of time it has increased its strength in contributing to domestic violence.

Some Ways Infatuation Works

You may have been living with your spouse for many years, and everything is going well with you. Its quite likely this one day you might begin to experience some difficult moments: maybe financial hardship, minor domestic issues, or just a moment of feeling loneliness. As you go through the experience, you may remember an old-time friend that you dated before you got married, and right then you made a friendly call to that person to ask how they were doing. In the back of your mind you may have stored some memories of things that you and your longtime friend did together before you got married, and as you converse with your old friend, your stored memories become fresh again, so you now begin to compare what you had many years ago to what you have now. Undoubtedly, you are feeling the desire to relight that old fire, and at the same time you want to stay with the marriage that you have. What you are now experiencing is a conflict; you are battling to manage two different intimate moments in your mind. Although you may not have physically regrouped yourself with your old friend, you will in some ways start depriving your spouse of some of his or her privileges, thus causing frustration that may take the long road to domestic violence. This deprivation may not be realized immediately, but as time passes, strange and possibly inappropriate behavior begin to surface, which indicate that something is missing and needs to be addressed.

Another way that infatuation takes place is through admiration. Sometimes someone may be admired by another of the opposite sex because of something they do, the way they conduct themselves, their personality, or their body structure; whatever the reason is for the admiration, it is possible for it to get to an infatuation level. The intertwining of relations at that moment does not necessarily mean that the two people are genuinely involved with each other and are ready to exchange marriage vows. Instead, they are only in love with what they see that they like, but they went ahead and got married anyway and live with each other until infatuation wears off. During the course of their married life, you may find both individuals becoming resentful, using inappropriate words to each other, and being ungrateful and abusive. It happens because someone became infatuated enough to force a marriage vow upon the other, and it's only common sense that if two people join in wedlock because of anything other than love, the marriage will suffer some turbulence that will rip it apart. To be able to conquer domestic violence in regards to infatuation means that there must be some aggressive adjustment and discipline made to keep the heart and mind grounded and properly focused. It is impossible to intimately manage two partners at the same time on the same level. It is improper and disrespectful to be calling the name of your old friend constantly in the presence of your spouse, and it is extremely ludicrous to fall for a flash in your eyes, something that is appealing for the moment. These are the kind of temptations that males and females are drawn into every day, but with a guarded heart they will mean nothing to a person, and once these channels of infatuation do not score any points, it can be assured that in this path of life, domestic violence will not have a chance to prevail.

Pull Down The Bar

In the very early centuries many homes built in America were built of a traditional design with a living room, a dining room, a den, and a kitchen. This was the way the layout of the majority of homes was until recent years. Some home owners who had these homes began to alter traditional homes to make a home alcoholic beverage bar, either in the den, the dining room, or in their renovated basement. I am aware that some of the alterations of the addition of a home bar give more beauty and value to the house, but just think of it while a wooden or brick structure was getting more beautiful and having more value, the human occupants of that same structure were living in some pain and agony of losing their physical beauty and values and living under the rubble of being demoralized constantly. I supposed that the idea of building alcoholic beverage bars in homes was for families and friends to have little social moments of drinking from the bars on special occasions such as birthdays, anniversaries, and other special moments, and also to keep the families from going to outside bars where they would be drunk and then have to drive home. I wish that I could say it's a great idea, but unfortunately I cannot because there is no sense in using coal to put out fire; it just doesn't work.

Yes, it is true that drinking liquor from your bar at home keeps you from going out and having to drive home drunk.My friends, while you are not doing that you are still in great danger of drinking excessively from your home bar and becoming heavily intoxicated because the liquor is just a step away from you. I am fully aware that you may say that you are in your own home so you can do anything you want to do. That may be so but is it worth the inflicting pain and wounds it cause to others.

In many homes where there are bars, usually one of the family members of that home has a very heavy drinking problem and because of the constant intoxicated habit, he or she exercises abuse and violence to the ones that are just occasional drinkers; the reason is easy access to liquor and without consequences.

A great number of domestic violence abusers started their first alcoholic sip at their own home, and that sip increased to many sips until the sippers are now able to drink one full bottles of alcohol per day. Soon the sips then become out of control and abusive habits emerge, from slapping to murder. Some homeowners may say that yes they have a bar in their house but it's not a big one. Others may say that they do not have a real bar, rather just a place where liquor is stored and many gather to drink in the basement of the house. Whether it's in the basement, the living room, a real bar, or a make-do bar, the fact is that the easy access to liquor in the house becomes breeding ground for domestic violence by alcoholic abusers.

If someone wants to win the battle over cigarettes, they cannot continue to purchase cigarettes and store them in the house. If one wants to win the battle over pornography, they will not win if they continue to sleep with pornographic materials in the house. Both cigarettes and pornographic materials will have to be divorced from the individuals in order for these battles to be won. It is amazing how willing people are to wear a cigarette patch to stop the smoking, how willing they are to stop attending night clubs in aid of stopping their drinking habit but how unwilling those same people are to tear down the drinking bar with all the liquor in the house. Quitting means quitting. It may take some time to get accustomed to quitting a habit but once the effort if made and actions are followed, the victory will be won.

If domestic violence by intoxication is going to be conquered, it means the beautiful drinking bars that are built in the homes must be pulled down and be destroyed. I do not recommend that the alcoholic beverage only get removed from the bar, because as long as the framework or the structural setup is still there, there will always be memories lingering and the temptation to restock is inevitable.

No one should ever underestimate the battle of turning their back on alcohol; it's one of the most challenging battles of addiction that mankind wrestles with, but the battle can be won and to do so is to completely wipe out every substance and memory of alcohol in the home, including totally dismantling and disposing of the house bar. If one can do so without any regrets, they are progressively winning the battle over alcohol and at the same time slowly but surely conquering domestic violence that is caused by the abusive use of alcohol.

A Better Funding Program

Anything we want to be effective enough to bring about changes cannot be done without adequate funding. We may have a great idea, a good plan, and highly skilled people to carry out the plan—that's all well and good—but the plan will never materialize unless it is properly funded. We know that money is not the answer to everything; however, money will help to find some answers to some things, and one of those answers is putting a lid on domestic violence with an aim to conquer it.

Many of the fights against domestic violence programs in America have been largely funded by private foundation from all over the American continent, but it seems as though there is not enough funding from Congress. I am not too sure of the reason for this, but I believe that every citizen of America should let their voice be heard in urging their members of Congress to support additional funding to conquer domestic violence since there are so many homes today where domestic violence has left either the mother only or the father only with the children in the home and in some case only the children are left because domestic violence has taken the lives of both parents.

A better funding program would provide better staffing wherever pockets of domestic violence programs are more frequent as well as training for victims and potentials victims along with better technological devices to curtail the violence.

Besides, many of the women and men that were victims of domestic violence are today still having a difficult time rising above their past experience. They feel so deprived of their lives that they haven't yet stepped out into the work force to find a job to help them better themselves .Because most of their adult lives were lived being physically beaten and robbed of their self-esteem, they currently do not even have a high school diploma to approach the job market with as a tool to start a new life. A better funding program for conquering domestic violence will enable the unfortunate victims to attend school and colleges where they could be better educated and more equipped in their various fields of study and recapture their images to enter and reenter the job market filed. There are no doubts that once an opportunity is given, not all will take advantage of it but some will, and it is a known fact that once people regain control of their lives, they tend to feel better about themselves and function better on their own.

I don't want to make a biased statement, but I am sure that almost everyone can agree that women are the ones that are mostly victimized by domestic violence, and the truth is, it doesn't matter where they were born, what they look like, what language they speak, or what color they are, none of them deserve to be treated in an abusive and violent manner by anyone. The question may be how would better funding could reduce the risk of domestic violence in a case where there are so many different barriers that women have to overcome individually?

One of the answer is that there are many more programs that can be put in place to help women cross over these barriers and get out of the mess, but due to lack of sufficient funds to carry out the programs, the programs are just formulated but cannot be activated. With such setbacks, women then are missing out on some important things that could help some of them to move on with their lives and not to get stuck in domestically violent environments.

Besides, children of the mothers of domestic violence are tired of watching their moms struggling and suffering in their environment. These children deal with the pain that their mother feels from day to day and even when they are with their friends at school and enjoying themselves, there are moments when their mom's pain strikes them deep in their heart and sadness is then felt. Some of the children are not able to talk about what they have seen happening to their mom, so after a long period of silence, they slip into depression. The end result of this is that whenever a person slips into depression, he or she usually is treated with anti-depressant pills for a long period of time and sometimes for the rest of their lives. If treatment is not given, then such person can become very violent and is considered a danger to society and must be placed into a suitable facility for treatment away from his or her family. We can almost say that a lack of proper funding for domestic violence helps to promote children unfairly being put on anti-depressant medication that could be avoided.

I know that this is not the direction that parents would like to see their children take in their lives, but it is one of the possible outcomes for children who have to live every day in a domestically violent environment where moms could hardly give a smile because ongoing of violent treatment.

The question that faces all is, would we rather see our future generations who have the potentials to be presidents of America and prime ministers of other countries, senators, city counselors, mayors, governors, and loyal citizens become ruined and not have a chance to reach to the highest level of their potentials because they were product of mom's domestic violence pain? I believe that more money should be invested in saving the children so that the evil of domestic violence gets weeded out.

I strongly suggest that every citizen, every private business, every charitable organization, and most important, the responsible government agencies, take more aggressive and financially supportive actions in providing better funding to conquer this violence and save the children from grief.

Volunteer Your Service

It is important to have the proper funding to be able to have a successful domestic violence prevention program, but the money may not always be available to fund this program, so other methods have to be incorporated to keep the program alive.

What is really at stake in a domestic violence environment are the lives of mothers , fathers, and young children who are not too sure of what the future holds for them, along with the pain and frustration felt by others when they learned that their relatives are involved in domestic violence. Inasmuch that money is needed to compensate for time spent in laboring at a work site, there comes a time when one must look beyond the monetary rewards and see other rewards. Not every domestic violence program will have a fully paid staff as they would want, but every domestic violence program needs a full staff to be effective. This means that some of the members of the staff would have to volunteer their time in order for the program to be successful.

Although volunteering may seem to others as a non-rewarding job, it is not so. Those who are put on a payroll may be paid every week or month and seem to be very satisfied because they know that after they have done their duty, they will be paid. I am sure that everyone does enjoys that check, but taking all things into consideration, I don't think anything can be more rewarding than to know that volunteer time has being used in saving many lives from being ruined in the web of domestic violence. Those who gets critical about volunteer time in a shelter for domestic violence should not. Instead, it should be looked on as time spent trying to be a good Samaritan. It must be remembered that the people that go into the domestic violence shelter have the same needs as those that are not in the shelters. They need jobs, counseling, housing, food, and help to improve some of the skills they went there with. Not all of these victims are getting a weekly pay check so that they can afford to pay professionals to provide these services for them. If they don't get the necessary services, some of them could find themselves running right back to that which they ran away from, and that will not be conquering domestic violence, so what's needed is for volunteers to find some time to help some victims and their families to stay out of domestic violence environment by offering their skills to domestic violence sites.

Accept No Trade-Off For Abusive Treatment

Quite often it is noticed that many victims after being treated in an abusive manner by their partner have tried to compromise their pain by accepting gifts or special treatment of some kind from their abusive partner as a means of appeasing the problem so that the victim does not call the police or report the abuser to the appropriate agencies. The special treatment may sometimes be a trip many miles away from home, enjoying a night out at the movies and possibly dinner, clothes shopping, or maybe a boat cruise for a few days. The abuser will possibly go out of his or her way to try other exciting things to cover up the mess except offering the victims an invitation to a couple's counseling session or an opportunity to attend a domestic violence program.

The unfortunate thing is that although some victims have physical marks on them that remind them of the violent abuse they suffer, with just a few enticing offers from their abuser, they mentally erase their wounds and fall for the offers. The dangerous part of this is that the abuser knows the weakness of the victim is accepting offers at any cost; therefore, the abuser will make it a habit in continuing to carry out violent and abusive behavior to his or her victim just because the victim mentally erases pain when exciting offers are made.

Obviously situations like those do not help to combat domestic violence. What victims fail to realized is, as long as abusers knows that they can get away with abusive behaviors, they will not stop abusiveness until the victims take some actions to make them stop. The truth is the end to abusive and violent behaviors by abusers are in the hands of the victims—whatever they settle for is what they will receive.

It would only be suicidal to be inflicted with internal wounds and use the therapy of trips, dinners, movies, and cruises to heal the wounds. Doctors never recommend external medication to take care of internal bleeding. Superficial excitement last but for a while, but internal bleeding, if not remedied, will last until the root cause of the bleeding is dealt with, and the root cause of domestic violence pain is the person who is causing the pain. Never should it be that a person is more in love with things than themselves, for in order to pass things for yourself and perhaps by yourself, you first must heal yourself, but if you destroy yourself to get things, what good are those things to you when you get them? I can assure now that they will be no good to you, so fix yourself before you become excited about getting things. I mean to tell you that the domestic violence treatment that you are currently experiencing must stop now; that is, you must find a way to effectively turn down the offers given to you before and after any abusive moment by your abuser. Be very firm and be very serious about "No" when those offers are made to you, for if you don't, you will only be helping abusers with their program and agenda.

I am fully aware that every domestic violence situation will not take the same approach; the abusers are all different. However, you, the victim, should be able to study your abuser in detail enough to know when and how is the best opportunity to have him or her be arrested by the proper law enforcement officials.

You must always remind yourself that you must conquer this violence today, not tomorrow, and bring an end to it so that it does not go on to someone else's son or daughter. If you can remind yourself of that, you will eventually find the motivation to make a start in doing something.

You may be one of the victims now that are saying "I don't see how I can say "No and be firm about it with the offers that my mate puts to me—I will be abused more" Ok, that's understood, but the pain you are feeling must stop, and your abuser must be taken away from you to stop this abusive pain. My recommendation is that you keep a journal of every abusive occasion in detail; be sure to have the time and date of each occurrence. If you feel it is safe for you to go to dinner with your mate, then you should consider going but with your journal. At some point during dinner you should try to use the restroom and at that point your cellphone in the restroom will help you not to accept any more trade-offs for abusive treatments. In almost every invitation that you get to go someplace with your abusive mate, there is a restroom there, and ninety percent of the times, there is some kind of access to phones. You can conquer domestic violence with turning down offers aggressively or not accepting them as trade–offs but using them instead to turn your mate in the right direction by putting him or her in the right hands for help.

Change Your Hangout Crowd

None of us should be surprised at the impact on our lives by the company we hang out with. We sometimes find ourselves talking the way they talk, acting the way they act, going the places they go, and believing the things they believe. We really don't realize this impact has taken a place in us until long after when we find ourselves either being told by people that something about us is not the same or we have pulled our self over off the highway of life and begin to evaluate ourselves because of something unrelated to what people think they see in us gone wrong. Very rarely, we try to face up to the truth immediately that there are some significant changes that have taken place in our lives. The reason we don't own up to the truth is because we know to ourselves what those changes are and the source that breeds them. Often we prefer to beat around the bush about the cause rather than put our finger on the pulse because we don't want what impacted our change to be removed from us, for we would be disturbing an ant nest and interrupting the comfort zone of other people's lives, so the best that we try to do is to leave well enough alone and just live with the condition that we find ourselves in, even though its unpleasant.

Let me bring your attention to this: if you hang around a pigpen every day feeding pigs, you may not talk like a pig, but you will surely smell like one. This is not because you choose to smell like one, but it's just the nature of the job. If you work in a liquor store, although you may not drink liquor, you will smell like liquor and have a potential to perhaps one day take a sip or two because of your environment. The fact is that you may not light the fire, but you have a strong smell of the smoke, and if you love the smell of the smoke so much, one day you will light a fire just to get smoke on you. Now we must understand that there are people with different mentalities about life that live in our world today. There are people that are very peaceful and would make every sacrifice to maintain peace. There are others that are very mild mannered that would be very peaceful up to a certain point in life, and there are those who speak nothing else but violence. These violent people express violence in every form and fashion that they can think of. My question for you is of these three behaviors, which one you would not want to associate yourself with? Now I am sure if I can answer for you, your answer would be "I do not want any association with the violent people."

Well, some domestic violence is engineered by the violent crowd that the perpetrator hangs out with. If a person is constantly hearing every day that the way to solve a problem with their mate is to slap, kick, shout, and carry out other violent and abusive actions towards them, one day that person is going to try it with his or her mate because that's the anthem that is playing in their head, and what is in the head will surely get to the hand.

How often have it has been noticed that many couples have spent many years of marriage together enjoying each other's company and after a while as soon as one of them began to hang out dedicatedly with perhaps some of the old-time friends or with someone who really cannot find purpose for their life, that mate comes home and begins a trend of abusive and violent behaviors? One cannot help but say that the company the mate hangs out with is a big influence in the change of the behavior.

We cannot escape the truth that a person is a product of his or her environment. If the environment is good, most likely the product would be good; if the environment is bad, then the product will be bad. I am very convinced that if some of the hangout crowds are changed, the level of domestic violence will drop. If your company are people who talk negative things about their mates, people who have no respect and regards for their mates, people who entertain abusive conversations about their mates, you should start to think about quitting that company. If you don't, you will only be planting a seed in you to do the same to your mate.

If you are in a company that is very controlling, domineering, and jealous of their mate, you should consider changing that crowd, for if you don't you may become the same to your mate, and if you become unsuccessful with your endeavors, you could cause a friction that affects domestic behavior.

If you are in a crowd that's in control of their mates, you must surely watch out for you may want to go home and disturb the smooth-running relationship that you have with your mate in the name of being in control and create an atmosphere for domestic violence. Let sleeping dogs lie; if you wake them up they might bite you.

Interestingly, the crowd you hang out with speaks very loud to you when you are not in their presence — their voices are still heard in your ears even when you are with your mates and during these moment some of the words and actions are passed on to your mates through you, whether it is positive or negative actions. To help conquer domestic violence, everyone should be extremely careful of the company they hang out with, for the company will either enriched your relationship with your mate to a very healthy level or break down your relationship with your mate to the level of domestic violence or worse.

Defeating The Intimidation Of Weapons

There are many people all over the world that have legal permission to carry a weapon (gun), maybe for the purpose of some business operation or because of they just feel that they must have one. Whatever the reason is, they do have access to a deadly weapon.

The people who do so are people who sometimes are living with spouses and at the same time are encountering marital as well as other domestic problems. Although in today's society guns are permitted to both male and female as a weapon for use when necessary, most of the times you will find that a large percentage of the ones who have access to guns are males. This is the same even with owners of business. It is not at all surprising to know that, since the traditional workforce and business owners in the past were comprised mostly of men but now has become more diverse with women. Traditionally more businesses today are passed on to more sons than daughters, so such conditions put more men in the position to have more weapons (guns) to their advantage than women would have.

When a man is given a weapon such as a gun to carry on him or to be kept in his custody at his business, he feels stronger than the power of ten very muscular men put together. His weapon makes him feel so safe that he throws his weight around vehemently and is not remorseful about who he may crush, whether that person is his mother or not. For some reason users or carriers of weapons seem to develop a big ego and very little compassion for others.

Regretfully, this mentality gets transferred to homes where wives who are faithfully and loyally serving their families now have to live with the intimidation of some weapon user shouting and pushing her around because there is a weapon of easy access in the house. Women who live in these environments act very scared and have a tendency to be antisocial, even though that's not their nature. They do so because in their minds they are uncertain of their future and fear for their lives. They very seldom come out of their homes to take a walk by themselves and if they do, they are walking with a demeanor that is unapproachable. What they are doing with such demeanor is making sure that no one has any interest in holding any conversation with them, for if they do, returning home to their spouse could become a federal case, that is, violent arguments. Is this the way for any human being to live? If your answer is "nothing is wrong with that," I beg to differ, I must say that such a life is nothing else but a person who is very seriously intimidated by weapons in their house and who allow their social environment to be dictated by arrogant weapon users.

We are all aware that weapons cannot hurt people by themselves; they would have to be used by individuals. You may suggest that one way of defeating intimidation of weapons is to remove the weapon from the individuals. It may work, but only for a while, for if you remove weapons from individuals, those same people can always find a way of getting more weapons in their possession, and the intimidating process only starts all over again. Sometimes we work around a problem hoping that we will solve it, but it doesn't get solved that way. We must, without compromise, place our finger directly on the problem to solve it, even when it hurts us the most.

If we are going to defeat the intimidation of weapons, it means that people who are licensed to have them in their possession should be made to allow unannounced inspections or visits by a weapon inspection officer. Also, weapons should be taken away from weapon carriers if on any occasion they intentionally used threatening words to their spouse in reference to their weapons. Women who live with spouses that try to intimidate them this way should never take threatening words for granted, for one never knows the things that are going on in the minds of others although it may be said "My husband is not serious." Once it begins with threatening words of intimidation, actions are most likely to follow, perhaps not immediately but eventually.

I realize that there are women who have lived like this and some who are still living with the threatening words, who will say "I pay no attention to him, he is always saying that." If you think that because you are accustomed to hearing it that everyone else in the house feels the same way as you do, that's a mistake because if you have young children, they feel very traumatized by the threats but are afraid to say anything to anyone.

It's never wise to live in a confined space with anyone who consistently makes intimidating remarks about his or her particular weapon. Someone in that space must leave to avoid physical altercation. If the person who is threatening refuses to leave, then the person whose life is under intimidation and threats should leave. I know that we all don't feel it's fair for someone to run us out of our space because of threatening words; that is true, but when you think of how much more flexibility you have away from the threats to pursue every possible measure to bring the intimidator under control, you would agree that it was a wise decision to leave. You do not necessarily have to get into a verbal or physical battle with someone to prove to them that you are not intimated by their weapon. Instead you should find other non-confrontational means to accomplish the same goal—defeating the intimidation caused by a weapon.

Under no circumstances should women tolerate weapons and weapon talk, swinging back and forth within a relationship. It doesn't matter how much they love these men and how very financially secure they feel. The truth is, they may be financially secure, but their lives and children are not. Every woman who has to deal with this kind of intimidation and fear should defeat intimidation by taking immediate action and doing what's necessary to protect their own lives and also their children and future grandchildren

Break Down The Walls

Almost everywhere around the world we find walls. Some walls are built to protect cities, some are built to support a particular structure, and others are built and served as dividing portions. For whatever purpose they are built, that purpose must be very positive, for if it's not, wherever they stand, they can create monstrous repercussions that can negatively impact a community, a city, a town, or a state, depending on the extent of the impact. Walls are sometimes built from materials that are not durable and can be easily pulled down or of materials that are very durable that can weather any storm without being damaged. Some walls are built in a short span of time while others may take many months to build and involve more work. Regardless of how strong or how weak a wall may be or whether it took a long time or a short time to build, the fact is, it's a wall, and it is placed wherever it is to send a message of some kind.

Isn't it quite amazing that if we see a wall built in a place that we think it should not be, we are ready to pull it down if the permission was given to us? We walk by very tall walls every day that are not outside in the communities but are in our homes, and the permission is given to us to pull them down, yet we leave them standing. Those walls are not the neighbor who wouldn't stop looking over in your yard or the kids who continually throw the ball over in your yard. You wish it was that because you can resolve that by building a very tall fence to keep the neighbor's eyes out and keep out the balls that get over in your yard. Unfortunately that's not so. The walls that are built up are walls of hostility, walls of resentment, walls of abandonment, walls of browbeating, walls of intimidation. These are some of the walls that are sitting right in the center of homes and between relationships that need to be blown down and leveled not be rebuilt again. They are the walls that have placed many men and women in prison as a result of domestic violence. They are the walls that have caused many families in domestic violence shelters, and they are the walls that reproduce a generation of domestic violence.

How do we conquer domestic violence with these walls still standing? Do we give up and say they have been there for a long time and there is nothing we can do? Do we continue to do business as usual and pretend that they are not present? Do we say "Oh, they will come down by themselves"? I am afraid that none of those approaches will ever work to conquer domestic violence. Just like these walls are built, they can be taken down and where none is built, connecting bridges can be built instead.

To really conquer domestic violence in pulling down walls that might have been built long ago, erected between couples, the approach is not to be like a mad man and make random strikes at walls. Doing so will only make matters worse; instead, start chipping from the top, that is deal with the current issues. That may not be the real cause of the affected wall, but as you deal with the present issue, you will eventually work your way to the foundation structure of the wall; that is the rooted cause of the reason you have a wall in the home. As long as you can get to the root, you can resolve the matter and recapture what you have lost for all those months or years.

If you don't have any wall affecting the relationship, you should take any vacant space and turn them into bridges. This means that you should seek to keep a regular connection in everything that you do with your mate, for by regular and close connections there will be no room left to invite and harbor destructive devices and behaviors for wall building. The work of connection is hard, but it's worth fighting for because it is one of the tools to conquer domestic violence.

My message to everyone today is if you have walls, get to work and start breaking them down, not tomorrow, or next week, but now, and if you didn't have a wall but have vacant space, build connecting bridges that breed better relationships that keeps out hostility, resentment, abandonment, browbeating and intimidation–little seeds that makes tall trees

Consult The Family

Many things that we do in our lives could be prevented before they even start, and what has started could be properly directed if the appropriate persons were contacted to give instructions and directions. Quite often we take matters into our own hands to do as we please because perhaps we become overwhelmed, we are on a panicking state of mind, or we just feel that we know the law of the land more that everyone else. Whatever the reasons are that cause us to take matters into our own hands, we should step back and proceed with caution when we find ourselves having to make that choice because we may sound right, look right, and may be have the right idea, but it was engineered the wrong way.

Many families engaged in potential domestic violence are digging deeper holes for themselves in the relationship, believing that they are conquering the situations but are really not; instead, they are inviting victimization. This is not to say not to take some common sense actions to help yourself from becoming a victim. Not at all am I indicating that; what I am indicating is that because domestic violence is such a crime that the levels are increasing daily, those who may be around it and are trying to conquer it should not do so without a family lawyer.

It's natural that sometimes when we are trying to get out of a situation, we do not look at the broader picture. All we are concerned about is "getting out"; then later the broader picture stares us in the face, and we then realize that we are not completely out, we only got out of one situation but still have more issues to deal with.

One of the reasons that a family lawyer should be consulted, especially if it's a family and not just two people is:

- What measures are going to be taken with the children
- What about properties
- Spousal support or alimony
- Continued payment of rent/mortgage/ college tuition
- Communication between the family after separation
- Necessary visits of children after separation

You may say that the court will decide all this when case gets there. You are quite right, but in the meantime, the concerns above are still concerns that must be dealt with whether or not the case goes to court. If the parties involved could work out their agreement without violent and abusive behavior it would be great, and then we could say that the power of good reasoning and understanding scored a big victory over domestic violence; however, ninety-nine percent of the time, that is not so. This is why it is so important to have the family lawyer involved because the involvement will allow the attorney to be the mediator instructing and directing the family in his or her professional wisdom and keeping everyone away from frictions of domestic violence. I am sure that the question "Who is going to pay a lawyer for all this?" will be asked.

My answer is would you rather spend the money to prevent the violence (conquering) or would you prefer to keep the money, permit the friction between both parties, suffer the violence, and perhaps burial, then look for an attorney. Which is better?

Off-The-Record Child Support

I am sure that there are many civil understanding with couples regarding separation. That is, many couples who have separated from each other to live at different location have agreed on their own terns together not to visit each other anymore for an agreed-upon length of time. They have settled that away from court, trusting each other that their words are sufficient to believe and that none of them would violate the trust. Is verbal or mutual understanding enough to feel secured and settled with an understanding?

Not always. Mankind has a tendency to make rules and violate them—even simple rules that he makes to discipline himself.

We must not be naïve in thinking that everyone who has to break off a relationship would do so with diplomacy. Not at all, because some people are very possessive and although they may verbally agree to end a relationship physically, mentally, they will not let go, so they try to find other means to stay in their separated mate's life just because they believe they still own that mate.

One of the measure that they use to encourage their possessive behavior in agreeing with their separated mate to allow them to bring to the house whatever amount of monetary child support they can whenever they can provide it, as well as visiting the child or children without any regulated or arranged schedule. You should not have to guess what the game is, but just in case you don't know, the game is to control whereabouts and monitor communications and social activities. These mates are considered slick stalkers; they are the ones who will have several relationships with others of the opposite sex and say its ok for them but although they know that your relationship with them has ended, they still want to tell you where you should go, who you should talk to ,and how long you should be on the phone. This is the main reason why they settle with you off-the-record or out-of-court child support arrangements, to be in your presence for monitoring purposes. Under these stalking conditions, it is only natural for the person who feels like their life is controlled by someone who they no longer have a relationship with to rebel, and the rebellion then escalates into violence that may at some stage affect not only both parents but also the child or children. It happens all because of off-the-record child support, which can be a big mistake.

How can one conquer this page of domestic violence?

The first thing I would like to discuss is that domestic violence is not something to toy with; it's very real and can be extremely fatal. Therefore, people who break off relationships with their mates without court action should be very direct and decisive with the off-the-record child support. If you have a very understanding and respectful departure, you can probably work alone with it, but whenever there is a possessive person involved, there should never be an off-the-record child support whatsoever because possessive mates cannot be controlled unless they are controlled by the law. Child support from persons with such behavior should always be through the mail.

The second thing is you the person who collects the child support must be very mindful of working on themselves because victims of domestic violence or victims of broken relationships carry a high level of anger. Every effort must be taken to control that. This is important because when a victim reflects back on their own life to see all the good times they had in early life and now look at the manner or method that he or she has to now use to support the children, frustration and anger could take over and get vented on the children. You may say that will never happen, but you might surprise yourself that it has already happened or it's happening now, and you don't realize it. Work on yourself and look forward, not backward.

If you can come to the truth of the risk involved with off-the-record child support, it will help you to make good judgments about what you should and should not do, and the good judgment will enable you to conquer domestic violence in child support.

Conquering Setups For Abuse

Domestic violence perpetrators are never tired of their practice. The violent behavior and abuse boosts their ego, and because they want to keep their ego boosted, they must find a way to carry through their programs without being in direct contact with their victims if they don't have to. Keep in mind that your abuser already knows some things about you. He or she knows your strengths and your weaknesses. They know what you are very good at and what you are not good at in terms of your skills. Having knowledge of these particular areas of your life, your abuser will set you up to fail in the very weak areas of your life in order to have a reason to abuse you or carry out violence.

For instance, if you are not too good on spending money, your abuser will give you money to purchase merchandise for yourself and use whatever is left to get something else for the children. The statement "whatever is left" does not state a particular amount; however, after you have done what you were told to do, your abuser will then let it be known to the children that he or she gives you money to specifically buy merchandise for the children and you did not. Of course that is not the truth, but that is what the children are going to believe.

Once this message get across to the children and the children see little or no shopping is done for them, it then causes them to turn against the target parent and violent or abusive behavior can then take place between the parent and children while the abuser sits and enjoys the show and violent moments of his/her victims. The fact is that you were premeditatedly set up by your abuser to suffer violence and abuse indirectly by your abuser.

If you are a person that suffers domestic abuse because of setups, you don't have to feel that you are always going to suffer this way; you can change this; you can conquer it. It just takes some willingness in you to want to make the adjustment. The first place to start is to overcome pride and take on a humble status. I mention this because whatever your weakness is, you are going to need someone to help you to strengthen that area, and pride could make you say no one needs to know your business.

Remember that you are not the only one that has a deficiency—everyone does, but some have a greater proportion than others, and some people are not truthful to themselves, so please don't let pride take you down. Allow yourself to be humble enough to get help from where it is possible to improve your weakness, not forgetting that your aim is to conquer your setups and avoid domestic violence. Once you work on your weaknesses and improve them, your abuser will notice after a few tries that you are no longer where you were a few months or weeks ago and eventually cease from the effort of baiting you because it is not working any more.

The next thing that you must do apart from being humble is be confident in yourself; tell yourself that you can change, you will change, and you have changed. These are important statements that you must tell yourself as often as you can because they will help you not to lose track of your goal and the reason for adjusting your life. If you fail to do this, you only fail to believe that you are making progress and can eventually slip right back to where you are coming from.

The efforts to conquer domestic violence and abuse by conquering setups requires hard and disciplined work, but the rewards are gratifying because victims of these areas can now say after the have overcome, they know the pain that comes with their different weakness, and they will be able to help others who are in those same situations.

Learn To Cope

In order to succeed in life, we all must learn to cope with some of the ups and downs that are generated from life. Those who have the experience of achieving an education regardless of what level it is know that you did not think well of some of the teachers or professors that taught one or some of your classes. You said they were jerks, and you did not believe that those professors knew what they were doing. Nevertheless you coped with what you called their ignorance and their unskillful method of teaching, all because you wanted to come out on the winning side of achieving an education. There were times when you felt like yelling at your professor, but you realized that the aggravation was only for a while. It would stop when the course ended.

I must tell you that even when you are the victim of domestic abuse and violence, if you are not careful you could, by retaliation to someone other than your abuser, become a supporter of domestic violence. This is likely to happen to people who cannot cope very well with certain situations. Let me speak to some of you now. Some of the mates that have abused you and were very violent to you have now gone out of your life. You have taken on a new direction in life, and so have they. Unfortunately, although you have resolved that relationship, it annoys you strongly whenever you see your ex-mate with his or her new mate and that new mate presumptuously sets him or herself up to tease you by putting on a romantic show with your ex-mate in your presence. Or even more annoying is to notice that your ex-mate treats his or her new mate like a queen or king.

The difficulties of physically experiencing this or learning about it could make a person forget everything that they can lose and get themselves engaged in a retaliatory mood of violence because their coping level is at zero.

So now the person who was once a victim of domestic violence has now become a suspect of domestic violence.

To be able to conquer domestic violence in this area (if this is the area that you have a battle with) you must learn to cope or how to cope.

This just means that if a person feels that their ex-mate is trying to belittle them, they should not stay where they are and be subjected to the insults and all the other teasing behaviors present. Instead, coping means you can remove yourself from environments that you believe would draw you into a confrontation with you ex-mate or with the significant person involved. Removing yourself doesn't say that you are a coward or that your ex-mate and company really got to you. What it really says is that you are the person with the better judgment, and until you are fully emotionally equipped to stand around and watch certain behaviors that do not impact you, you chose to excuse yourself.

Such action is a very intelligent way of conquering domestic violence because it takes two people to make a quarrel or pull off a fight, and by leaving the scene of an environment that can turn into domestic violence, you have defeated the evil plot; you have conquered the moment with your wisdom. You will not be always removing yourself from a scene like this; it's only until you are emotionally strong enough to deal with it, and you sure will be eventually, but in the meantime the coping method of removal will help you to be strong and keep you from being a suspect of domestic violence.

This method of removal may not be conducive for every ex-mate. There are other ways to cope such as occupying the mind with other things that are beneficial or listening to music as a form of ignoring teasing moments or violent temptations. There are several kinds of approaches that can be used. However, whatever approach one wants to use, the message must be coping to conquer domestic violence, and the person coping must know that if they fail to cope, they could be drawn into domestic violence, but once they cope well, they have won the battle over being drawn into domestic violence conflict with a senseless ex-mate and company.

Should This Child Ride In Another Man's Car?

A major element of domestic violence today, especially among teenage moms and dads, is that of having the child of the departed father riding in the vehicle of another man that mom seems to be finding some interest in. Some fathers live a very self-centered and manipulative life; they know that the relationship between them and their child's mother has ended, but because they want to manipulate the welfare of their child's mother, they put strong sanctions on the mother, informing her that she must not put the child in another man's vehicle.

This may sound to some of you that the father has the right to say what his child can and cannot do. To some extent it is justifiable, but when a situation is used to manipulate and control another person's life, it is not justifiable because the motive is wrong. Many of these dads who are putting these demands on the mother will not give any extra money to the baby's mother for her to get bus fare or even pay a taxi to take the child around to important appointments, yet they want to call the shots from a distance with a twenty-dollar support allowance.

If you are in a position like this one as a mom, you know how unreasonable and unrealistic this type of demand is. As a mother, you have your child and should do whatever it takes to serve the child's best interest, but in the meantime, you and your child may have to endure some changes to continue on in life since dad chose to go a different way. Doing so could make dad feel like he would have to resort to violence since he cannot get his demands met. The violence may not only affect you but the child as well as the persons whose car you may be carrying the child in.

The question now is how this element of domestic violence could be conquered.

Let me start with the ladies who are currently involved in a relationship like this. Ladies, you should never sit back and wait for that father of your child to change, to say that you have conquered the situation. Although changes are available to everyone, that man that you are waiting upon to change may never change; therefore, you must take matters into your own hands and begin to take some actions. I am sure that men with such a manipulating mentality do at some point show some kind of threatening behavior or use words to you that are threatening when they cannot get what they want done. Moms, you should never sweep these threats under the rug and believe that they are not going to happen; they will someday. Now, begin a procedure that involves even some family members of your baby's father. Ask them to give him some wise counseling that would help keep him from endangering his child and his own life. If that is not working, get the community experts involved to give some advice and direction before you consider other legal steps. Remember that men who gravitate to such behaviors are not all trying to be nurturing about their child being in another man's car. When you have done all that you can and nothing works, you may have no other choice than to seek for an order of protection for yourself and your child. I know that it may sound very cruel, but that is not the intended motive. The whole idea is that most men in such a state of mind fail to listen to family members and other representative staff; therefore, their stubbornness will bring them under the law of the land. To prevent further affliction to themselves and to the lives of others, it would not be surprising to learn that many men would not agree with that method of preventing domestic violence, and that is expected because they possibly were never put in a position to experience manipulation like most single women with children do. Nevertheless whether or not it's understood by the men who oppose the actions, mothers who are left to raise their children without the father's physical support must exercise every option possible to raise their sons and daughters in a safe and secure environment that would conquer the onset of domestic violence.

To all the ladies who are not at all experiencing a manipulative environment with the departed father of your children, I would advise that you cherish what you are doing to prevent the situation. Perhaps you have something that is working, so study it well and see how much more you can do to improve it. Meanwhile, do not ignore the experience of other unfortunate ladies. A good suggestion is to talk to some of the other ladies to get an idea of what brought them to the position they are currently in. Their experience may be able to help you to better position yourself to prevent the onset of domestic violence between you and your child's father, and if for any reason you see it coming, you will be better equipped with information that will help you handle it.

I believe that every woman would like to have the cooperation of their children's father in a case of departure from the home (that is, the father is no longer in a relationship with the mother). The fact is, you cannot put a mind into a person; therefore, you do not know if a person is going to change and when they are going to. So you must live with an open mind and store as much information as you can in your mind, for you may need it later.

Discourage Laboring For Government Benefits

The word freeloader is a popular word that gets tossed around and it's attributed to people who always seek to get something for nothing and who eventually seek the opportunity to take from others but never give anything back in return.

There are some very strong men in every part of the world who are not handicapped, not physically or mentally disabled in any ways, but rather are very capable of holding down a job, have great potential to aspire, but refuse to work and earn a living because they could access the government benefits (food stamps and free housing) from their wives or girl-friends who are beneficiaries of government support

To have a man in your life that is not adding to you but taking away from you could almost be compared to robbery on the highway, especially if the man is taking from you with demands.

I know that our society today has moved away from what is called the traditional family life and has given way to a more liberal family life, but the biblical truth will never change; it remains true, and our ancestors have demonstrated the fact, which is, a woman was never supposed to provide for the man, but the man for the woman. Somehow throughout the ages something got twisted, and today we now find a large number of women are out in the workforce working while the men are home shacking up watching T.V. and sleeping. Or, we can find many women putting their pride away and is now collecting food stamp and other benefits from their governments while the men they are with premeditates to stay at home and become an indirect recipient of these benefits.

It is true that everyone choose whatever lifestyle they want to live and accommodate whatever living conditions they want, but the danger of having a man feeding off of the benefits is that after a while he gets comfortable to the point where he believe the benefits belong to him and not to the woman and the children. One should know what to expect in this case. It will be nothing else but a battle for ownership of the benefits , and as a result of this battle, domestic violence is the outcome. It happens all because the men are condoned by their baby's mothers to stay at home and not work but live off the benefits for the mother and children granted by the government. You may say, so what? If the women are comfortable with it, then no one else should worry about it. The issue is not that anyone is worried so much as it is about a choice not to work and to feed off of someone else's bread. The real concern is that doing so only creates a breeding ground for violence in a home. I am aware that many women encourage male counterparts of previous relationships in their home for security or for other reasons that are not beneficial to them, but realistically no female should fool themselves by doing so, believing that all is going to be well. You cannot prevent or conquer domestic violence when you are at the same time setting the stage for a conflict in your home. You should take some courage and tell your significant other who wants to live off of your benefits that you care about him but you first have to care about yourself and to do so is to have him stop depriving you and your child or children of the benefits you are getting to take care of yourself and your child or children. The risk of not doing so can be the loss of benefits, thus further causing hunger and anger to develop, but the rewards of doing so break tension and anger that in many cases are the lighted coal that fuel domestic violence.

You can conquer domestic violence by taking such courageous action or you can encourage domestic violence by doing nothing and allowing yourself to become a harborer. Whatever method you choose to use to address the situation of harboring, your aim should be to conquer and prevent domestic violence. It must be understood that the apolar is just as bad as the thief.

Boot Camp Will Give You Some Ideas

Domestic Violence Boot camp ideas:

Talk about it—before the relationship

Too often women get themselves into hostile relationship with men because they did not ask a very important question, which is "Are you a violent man?" or "Do you have a history of mistreating women?" Don't get smothered by that well-dressed man, looking very muscular, speaking very eloquently, driving that S class Mercedes Benz, working in a management position for some big company, and making the world of promises. The important question of violence and mistreatment towards women must be answered before any commitment of relationship.

Disagree sometimes as a test

If you intend to be in a relationship with a man that you really don't know, it's good to disagree with him sometimes. You will have an idea of the product that you will be getting. Not everyone can disagree and keep a calm composure. Some men gets into a rage, especially to know that person who disagrees with them is the person who they think is supposed to listen to them. The rage they get into shows every evidence of escalating into a fight. Ladies, you can find that out early before you commit to relationship.

Cancel a few dates

Dates are important to men. They look forward to escorting their intended wives to dinner, movies, musical entertainment, and other things during their time of courtship. Because these are very sentimental moments for individuals, ladies, you can get carried away and not know what the flip side of cancelling a few dates would be like with your intended husband. Therefore, you should cancel a few dates to give you a preview of dates in the future. When you do so, keep a close watch on the man's attitude, but more important on the words that comes from his mouth in reference to the cancellations. Ladies, by this time you will have an idea of which direction to go.

Find Out About Any Alcohol And Drugs Association

Alcohol and drugs abuse is one of the leading cases of domestic violence. Ladies should not just settle with the words of a man who said he does not use alcohol or drugs; she should find a way to test him in order to be sure of it. If he fails the test, it could mean that there could be future potential for domestic violence because of alcohol abuse.

The idea of boot camp in a man is not to provoke him but to help women from walking into violent relationships that can cost them their lives or living in misery for an unknown length of time. I am not implying that all relationships that started without any problems are without violence or violence-free. That's not the case at all. What I am stating is if we want to help to conquer domestic violence, it's time for women to step up to the task of asking men some specific questions, put them through some relationship boot camp before they could make a decision of having them in their lives. In other words, domestic violence could slow down if women decide not to settle for non sense with men but to be more specific with the approach.

Today domestic violence shelters are filled with women who "should have, could have, and would have." The mistakes that have been made are speaking very loudly, and domestic violence shelters now are overrun with the impacts of those mistakes. The children and other family members involved are also paying a heavy psychological price for those mistakes, and sadly the cemeteries all around the world are engraved with results of these mistakes.

The question now is how much longer we all can allow the impact of ignorance to sneak through our future generations of women. I believe it can stop now. It can be stopped with boot camp training. Yes, women, you need to act, and putting that man through some examination, you will find out through your boot camp if he is any kind of man at all. You should not feel any fear in doing so, for if you lose him, then you weren't supposed to have him, and if he comes through the test, there is a possibility that you may have a fruitful future with him. However, do not avoid boot camp; it can save your life from domestic violence.

Men Must Report It

For a very long time men have been victims of domestic violence, but it is very difficult for the appropriate authorities to step in and help to conquer the violence with them because men consider themselves to be macho; therefore, they would rather live with the pain and keep their macho status than to report it and feel like a wimp. Also, most men do not tell their friends about it, fearing that they would be laughed at for their cowardly position.

I wish that staying silent would prevent the violence or would stop the furtherance of it, but it does not. Men, you should understand that to be abused by a woman doesn't mean that they have changed their apparel to that of a male. It should be known that violence has no preferred gender, and some females like some males are strikers and cannot keep their hands to themselves, but specifically feel powerful when using their hands on a man or abuse him in other ways since men are considered to be the physically stronger gender.

To help prevent domestic violence men you must:

- You must drop the macho mentality and report your perpetrator.
- You must stop it soon so that your son doesn't feel like that is the way life is and that's normal.
- You must quickly look for the signs of violent women and move away from them.
- If you cannot contact the police, be sure to contact a domestic violence center and have them remove the violence from you.
- Don't run the risk of entering another relationship before you are healed completely.

If you keep quiet and do not report your perpetrator, you may cause your perpetrator to enter into another relationship at some point in her life and do the same thing, so the best thing that you can do for yourself and your perpetrator is to report any abuse you feel and help prevent the spread to another man.

A Tour Of The Body

By choice, some of you might want to tour your body and stop at all the marks and broken or fractured bones that domestic violence has left on you. Your touring is not to be proud of the scars but to help your sons and daughters of the next generation not to live what you have lived but to conquer the violence before it gets started:

- A tour of the head: are there any fractured bones of the nose? Do you have to continually wear sun glasses because of a damage eye? If you have, do you stop and think about it?
- A tour of the hands: are there any fingers broken? Do you have stitches from a weapon used on you? If you have, do you stop and think about it?
- A tour of the rib cage: Do your ribs hurt when you breathe? Was there a massive blow given to you across your rib cage that makes you have difficulty in breathing? If so, have you stopped to think about it?
- A tour of the buttocks area: does the area hurt when you sit down because of the constant kicks you suffered there? If so, have you stopped to think about it?
- A tour of the ankles: are any of your ankle bones constantly swollen or occasionally swollen as a result of you trying to run away from your perpe-trator? If so, have you stopped to think about it?
- A tour of the vital organs of your body: are there any kidney failures, heart problems, lungs, stomach, hypertensions because of the constant stress your body went through for fear of the next session of abuse by your perpetrator? If so, have you stopped to think about it?

Now that you have completed your tour, you do have a lot of regrets but at the same time you have learned a lot of lessons.

If you are comfortable enough to share your experience of abuse with your son or daughter, you should do so with the focus of letting them know that they should never stay in a relationship that compromises their well-being.

If they are not yet into a relationship, they must let it be known to their intended spouse the first evidence of abuse or violence will be the beginning of the end of their relationship and mean it. Let your child or children know that the mistake you made was to wait too long to end the relationship, and in waiting you were promised better days, but things only got increasingly worse. Let your child or children know that the way to conquer is to take early action and not to wait until after the pigment of your body becomes another color and your internal organs are malfunctioning along with many other physical and mental complications that can undermine their life before they can end the relationship. Avoid a disfigured body tour by conquering the violence early.

Close The Gap

Amazingly many relationship that start out very good and look really promising have now found themselves among the piles of the ones suffering domestic violence. These relationships surprise many because they show no indication of any signs of domestic violence. What's wrong then? There must be an unnoticeable problem somewhere. We very often hear the saying "It's not what you did that really matters; it's what you didn't do." Prior to marriage, couples stuck very close to each other during their phase of dating. They sometimes are on the phone a dozen times a day talking to each other, going out to movies together, and going on dinner dates and many other activities and events they attend together. Because they were always together, sometimes they give the public the idea that they never parted from each other. During those moments of dating and closeness they have with each other, they become very bonded, so their bond leaves no space between them for any thought of distancing. They stay very focus and very close because they were always doing things together. I am sure you could imagine the enrichment of their lives and the gap between them was so close that the thought of domestic violence and abuse was a foreign thought and anything that would invite pain would be quickly resolved, for the company of each other during those years was like heaven on earth. Each person was very special to the other. We wonder sometimes what causes the wheels of some of these relationships to spin backwards. Although we can find many things or many people to put the blame on, the underlying problem rests on what wasn't done; that is, the gap wasn't kept close; after a while, it was left open, so it created a distance for other intruding influences and problems leading to domestic violence .

A very common thing that happens during this experience is that both individuals accuse each other of a noticeable change that occurs but very rarely do they address what caused the change. In fact, if they do, one usually tells the other that he or she has issues. No one should ever underestimate the damages that are possible with distance in relationship. I am not referring to geographical distance; what I am referring to is the distance that comes about between two people living in the same house, sleeping in the same bed, eating at the same table but yet having no relationship. This is without any doubt a recipe and breeding ground for domestic violence. The violence does not start all at once; instead, it may begin with making simple issues in the marriage become very complex and cause aggravation that activates bad temperamental responses.

Certainly some of the behavior could be corrected, but the scars of what went wrong linger on and something that could have been prevented now has to be corrected.

There are no perfect marriages but many times domestic violence could be prevented by eliminating distances in relationship and closing the gaps in relationship. This can be done by using some of the following recommendations.

Effective communication: Be sure to talk to your spouse about things that you may have encounter during your daily routine, those things may be negative and positive, but regardless of what they are ,share them and keep the conversation interesting. If you have a thought, share that also and be ready for a response. At times you can be very humorous, but don't go overboard. You should make it a habit to laugh even when the joke is not all that great because doing so shows you enjoy communicating humor to your spouse. If you sense a slight breakdown in communicating, don't wait for your spouse to restart it; you take the initiative because the idea is not to keep a check on whose turn it is to start but to be sure that distance gap of communication is closed. Let your conversation be uplifting, inspiring, humorous, and loving.

– Be Sensitive: Be sure not to agitate your spouse in a particular sensitive area. If you know that your spouse has a certain discomfort level with something, let him or her know that you are aware of the discomfort and that you will do your best not visit those areas. Let them know also that you would like to be signaled in some way if you were to be found crossing that discomfort lines, whether consciously or subconsciously.

– Compliments: it doesn't matter who compliments you on things you have done, clothing that you wear, or fragrances that you put on your body; it is definitely not the same as the compliment that comes from your spouse. Be sure to tell your spouse that the clothes they are wearing look great. The job or task they are doing is wonderful and that you are very proud of all of their achievements. Your complimentary comments will make a strong bond between you and your spouse and brings more confidence in your relationship.

– Physical Exercise: Sometimes talking and having conversation is healthy for the gap to stay closed, but other times it's something else that's needed. It's caressing and embracing. Be sure to embrace your spouse at times; just a physical touch sometimes is all that is needed to reassure your spouse of your loyalty, your love, and your commitment to him/her. The actions that you do will speak louder than the words you say.

– Accepting Correction: age sometimes tells us that we don't have to listen to anyone correcting us when we are wrong because we are not children anymore. I do not advise that anyone should be carried with that; it does nothing else but put a dent in relationships and create domestic violence. Be willing to hear your spouse tell you that you are wrong about something and accept it with love.

Men, you should not feel so macho to the point where you do not want to hear your wife say to you that you are wrong. Neither should you women feel that that you are being trodden upon because your husband has to tell you that you are wrong. There can't be anything much better in a relationship than having both husband and wife live in submission to each other.

I cannot say that these are all the things you have to do to keep the relationship gap close to prevent and conquer domestic violence, but I can surely say that these may be some of the things in some particular relationships that never were done that create distance and allow room for domestic violence. Now you don't have to question anymore; just close the gap by using the recommendations above that you never used before.

More Accountability For Offenders

Another reason for the increase of domestic violence, is because offenders are not held accountable enough after they have served time in prison and are released; it is quite natural that if a person commits a crime and knows that the consequences are light, that individual is prone to commit another of the same type of crime again or perhaps worse. But if the consequences are very heavy, there is a lesser chance of that person committing the crime again.

What perpetrators of crime have done is to make prison a walk-through. In other words, prison wasn't tough enough to break them, so they don't mind repeating the same crime because they tell themselves that it will just be another walk-through, and when they get released, a rose garden awaits them on the outside. It is true that there are some disciplinary programs in place for ex-offenders of domestic violence but the real question that needs to be asked is how effective are they? If programs are in place just for the sake of going through the motions and they are not working, then they should be revised. Any program in place should have a sting that not only delivers some type of discomfort for the ex-offenders but helps to sober them up as they find their way back in society conducting themselves as normal citizens.

How could anyone justify a domestic violence offender slashing his or her girlfriend's/boyfriend's car tires, slapping the victim, spending six months in prison and returning to repeat the crime two weeks after release from prison? Well, the only thing that can be seen with that kind of looseness is that something is definitely wrong with the accountability process.

I am sure that every country has an accountability program for domestic violence offenders, but when offenders could breach their duties of accountability and run off to commit more acts of domestic violence, it means that the method of accountability needs a change. There should be an increase of time for probation visits. That is, more days should be mandated for offenders to visit their probation officer, and the length of time should also increase. This change will not change everything, but it might change some things. At least it will take away some of the free time that offenders have to get them into more mischief, and reducing their potential for mischief helps them to overcome and conquer the thoughts of repeating the crime.

Besides increasing the time of visiting the probation officers, offenders should have a specialist working with them to find jobs. Yes it is true that they should be looking for themselves since they don't need any help when they are about to be abusive. The goal is not to render evil for evil but to conquer any area where domestic violence can show up its claws. We must admit that some of the domestic violence offenders carry out their behavior out of frustration of not being able to find a job. As a result they become angry with the immediate person around them, and with relentless time they then get their show on.

– Finding a job therefore diminishes the potential for domestic violence in more than one way.

The time spent on the job takes away from time to become violent at home.
- Jobs sometimes have a way of motivating people to want to choose a better life—the focus of the offender could become a more family focus.
- Certain jobs are great tools to lead on to develop certain skills that occupy the mind.
- Jobs are wonderful tools to help to talk about your frustration of life and the regrets of the things you have done.
- Monetary benefits of jobs help to relieve some domestic financial burden that leads many to domestic conflicts.

Once there is a good accountability program for offenders, there is a better chance of offenders reshaping and refocusing themselves and a closer monitoring recorded is provided. The importance of this cannot be stressed enough for with a good accountability program many lives would be saved. For instance, if an offender did not meet his particular appointment with his/her probation officer, an accountability program could be in place that would immediately send an alert of some kind to the offender's previous relationships granting automatic security to his/her ex-counterparts. It is not saying that every time an offender does not show up to an appointment with a probation officer that he/she went back to revisit the last place of aboard to do more damage. That's really not the statement I am trying to relate. However, because the nature of mankind is to revisit his last place of aboard when he cannot explore new avenues, it is reason to believe that an offender will go back to his or her victim to be dangerous when there is not a new person to abuse.

Given all these reasons, there should not be any hesitation of having more and better accountability for it's to the benefit of the court, the offender, and the victim.

Reduce The Caseloads

What else could be worse than having a burnt out, highly stressed probation office working on a case and fall asleep over his file? One that's not too sure of how many appointments his client missed with him or losing track of court dates for his client? This can be an extremely dangerous risk taken, but it does happen when probation officers are overloaded with cases that make them not manageable and ineffective.

The overwhelming volume of caseloads in the hands of probation officers has caused offenders not to be properly monitored, and the poor monitoring techniques only open up cracks in the system for offenders to run off and commit more crime. It is by no means inconsiderate to the court to say that because domestic violence offenders are considered very dangerous that every measure should be taken to ensure that no probation officer is overloaded, and high turnover of officers should be avoided. To control such problems means that courts would need to hire more probation officers to reduce the caseloads, and more financial and technical support should be given to these officers in the check-in stations. If cases are poorly managed or poorly structured, then the lives of victims becomes more jeopardized, and everyone else associated with those victims has to work harder to protect those victims because the probation program failed.

The loss of a person in society cannot be replaced. While another person could fill a position that becomes vacant, the individual is unique and cannot be reproduced.

Knowing the value and importance the existence of human life, it is important for the probationary system not to be negligent in equipping officers with what's necessary to allow better maneuvering in handling offenders.

Every day domestic violence offenders are being arrested prosecuted and convicted then later released from prison and assigned to a probation officer. Whenever a probation officer is assigned to an abuser, the officer becomes responsible for investigating and evaluating the offender .He is to assess his/her potential risk of danger to public including his/her victims and to develop a probation plan that will work for the individual.

The probation officer also has the responsibility of constantly monitoring the offender to ensure that the probation rules are not violated, including staying away from any further violent acts against the victim.

Along with all of that, the probation officer makes recommendation to the court based on the offender's compliance with the probation rules. Looking at this picture, if you have too many caseloads assigned to a single probation officer, you don't have to calculate the chaos it will cause on the street or in homes when offenders are not carefully managed. The everyday occurrence of this violence creates heavy caseloads for probation officers, and the lack of being unable to keep up with the supervision of frequent occurrence of such crime has resulted in the courts using the same small and traditional crew to combat a very increasingly large and complex problem, and of course that will never work.

If the court cannot hire more probation officers to reduce caseloads because enough money is not available, then the court should consider promoting public awareness and general safety or some type of ventures. That incentive could involve a tax break, a scholarship fund, or some other opportunity wherever incentives are offered when money cannot be the rewarded portion. This way, many people would tend to get involved and dedicate themselves to the task.

Part II

Chapter IV

Can Religion Do It?

People have used religion to cover up their pain, their anger, their wickedness, and their abusive behavior. Some have managed to endure under the cloak of religion longer than others, but at the end of it, victims do report their long hidden pain because it's only so long that religion can hide feelings.

It is the practice of many criminals, including domestic violence offenders to use religion as a cover-up to make believe that their abusive behavior has changed when they have been granted released from prison. Careful evaluation must be given at this stage, for one can be dealing with the following:

A person who only goes to church, puts up the best behavior that they can, carries out the golden rule as much as they can, but only to do these things for a short while.

The reason for all this is to gain acceptance back in their victim's life. They want to convince their probation officer that they have really changed so that they can have less monitoring put on them, and they want to convince the community that they are Mr. or Mrs. Goodie Two-Shoes. Their aim is to win the trust of the general public, so they do some religious fronting for a short while. I do not mean to state that everyone who finds themselves in a religious setting after release from prison is a con artist. That not so, because there are some people who associate themselves with religion because they really want to change to a more productive life. The fact, however, is that some will use religion to gain acceptance so that they can repeat their violent behavior against their victim and others while those who really desire change soon find out that religion is only a pathway, for nothing else can make a person change his/her cruel habits except if he or she has a change of heart. Right in the heart is the fuel station for all wicked devices and all domestic violence. Offenders begin their violence at the station of the heart before they act it out on their victims.

Besides, offenders who use religion to hide their evil also encourage their victims join a religion hoping that by doing so the memory of their pain will dissipate after their abuse. That type of message is completely deceptive, for one could be comforted and soothed down of the hurts they feel in domestic violence, but after a moment or several moments of comfort, the pain is still there and is there only because the heart, where all the issues are, has not being dealt with. So, if both the offender and the victim of domestic violence are looking for religion to resolve their domestic violence issue, whether to disguise themselves under it or to dissolve the pain with, I must tell you now, that will not work. We should ask ourselves these questions:

- Who is our greatest enemy— the answer is ourselves.
- Who has the power to resolve the wickedness of our hearts—the answers is ourselves.
- What is the cause of the domestic violence—the answer is an evil heart.
- Where must healing begins for forgiveness to be granted—the answer is in our broken hearts.

As we take a look at the questions and answers given, we should note that in order to conquer the pain and the violent behavior of domestic violence in spite of everything else that can be tried, the answer is that there must be a transformation of the heart, not the cover of a religion. Don't think I am suggesting that you take your heart out and put another one in. That's not the case. What I believe will change the heart of every offender and victim is the changing grace of GOD that has the power to put everything that is right or wrong in the right place and bring both offenders and victim to peace with themselves.

I give credit to all the programs, the efforts, the neighborhood watches, the inputs by individuals, the courts, police, religions, and everything that any and every one tries to do to bring justice to offenders and protect victims of the violence, but these are just temporary solutions. I do believe that hardly anyone wants to have something temporarily fixed if they can find a permanent solution to the problem. Is there a permanent solution? Yes there is; it is where all offenders and victims come, to the place of having a personal relationship with GOD, the creator of heaven and earth, and submitting to his authority in their lives, but all of this must take place in the heart. When this happens, the offender will surrender his cruelty, and the victim will be healed from hurts. Religion must send the key message.

I do realize that everyone has their preferred religion that they believe in, and as far as each person is concerned, each preferred religion is the right religion. Unfortunately, I am not referring to religion here to conquer domestic violence because religion, again, cannot do it. Domestic violence is an evil spirit that takes up residence in the heart of men and women and can only be driven out when the heart and mind is at peace with GOD.

Use this conquering weapon that gets very little attention in our society, "the importance of a changed heart." That's the key message. I strongly recommend it, for it has never been known to fail. It is the best weapon for fighting against domestic violence and should take preeminence over every program, counseling sessions, prison, neighborhood watch, meeting, small and large group gatherings, conference, and workshop. This is perhaps the main course meal that will conquer domestic violence—not religion but salvation. This the message that must be sent.

The Message Must Be Right

The message to conquer domestic violence from religious leaders should:

– Not be confusing—but plain and simple
– Not be competitive—that is, no religion should be competing with another to determine who can bring the best message
– Not stressed on religion but on salvation
– Not be hidden from some but delivered to all
– Not be trusted into the hands of novice but by qualified and capable men and women who understands the call of the time.
– Bring hope and assurance to the hearers and heal the wounds that are open
– Not be limited to particular genders but offer help to all, regardless of what gender brings the message
– Be given with compassion for those afflicted by domestic violence
– Be reliable and consistent
– Urgent, yet cautious

The aim should be in the hearts of all religious workers that "people need deliverance from domestic violence and the main place of deliverance is in the heart."

Global Awareness

Although we know domestic violence is widespread all over the globe, there is still numbness to the violence in some countries around the world. It is not that victims of domestic violence do not understand the aggressive abuse and cruelty that is being done to them; they do know because pain is something that is felt by everyone when it comes. The fact is that some people are not educated enough to know what to do, so they settle for it as though it is a part of what comes with a relationship.

Global awareness is important because it will help to change behaviors in people before they travel from one country to another, whether or not they will be taking up residence in that country or visiting on business trips or for other reasons. The more informed a person is about a subject, the better the disciplinary measures are.

Keep The Children Safe

Children do not go to domestic violence; it comes to them and breaks their heart before they can get a chance to develop their individuality. If you as a parent find that your child is constantly getting exposed to the violence, take action quick to save your child's soul, body, and spirit—your child's self-worth.

Revoke The Weapon License
Turn The Weapon In

There are many who have a license to carry a weapon, possibly because of business or other reasons. In addition, the license may have being granted before such person began having domestic issues in their lives. Granted that the license were given before the onset of domestic issues occur, now that the person is experiencing domestic problems, all licenses should be suspended indefinitely, and weapons should be turned in to the appropriate government or city agencies. The action is not meant to be mean-spirited but to protect the individuals from unnecessary harm.

Report Suspicious Stalkers

People stand around at street corners, in parking lots, bus stops, and train stops pretending that they are busy doing something, but in actual fact they are doing nothing else but stalking their ex-mates. Sometimes it is easy to tell who these people are because whenever they see you watching them, they begin to show signs of nervousness or get very agitated at your stare at them.

When you notice such behavior, report the suspicion immediately; you probably may be saving someone's life. You may not always be right, but rather than doing nothing and regretting it later, it's better to make a phone call and feel at ease—when in doubt, make a call.

What The Future Holds

As we examine the current situation of domestic violence and notice the rampant outbreak that is now occurring all over the world, no one should deny the fact that the battle to conquer domestic violence will be an uphill battle, but with consistency and commitment, the task can be done. The different life-style, habits, and behavior that have now infiltrated our society has made the fight more intense than it was twenty years ago. Our society is one of a gullible nature. If something looks good, feels good, and promises well, we swap it off immediately without testing it. We are no longer satisfied with what we have; we want more and would give up faithfulness for unfaithfulness.

What is wrong with the faithful husband you have, the faithful wife you have? Just because someone else from around the corner looks good smells good, and talks good, is your faithful spouse worth exchanging and suffering abuse for that? I don't think so. Have you any proof of the pudding that you want to taste? Do you know anything about him or her? I'll bet you don't know enough. What a way to go—all roads lead to domestic violence.

Our society today lacks self-control, reasoning power, and thankfulness. We prefer gullibility over faithfulness and superficiality over inside qualities. Our world is upside down: right is now wrong, and wrong is now right. Our world, for the most part, is an exposed one. Fashion has dictated our sexuality. Our females feel sexy looking if they can dress half naked, well tattooed and reveal certain private parts of their bodies. Our male eyes and mind are blown out of our heads to such excitements. Doesn't all this provoke the action of domestic violence? Oh yes, for the lust of the eyes looks later for fulfillment of the body and after that passes, which is at least thirty minutes or more, then the unfulfilled promises made turn to violence and abuse.

Hey! What about the hostility that our society gives off today? The yelling, the sharp answers, and coldness we show to each other. What we must understand is that our environment almost everywhere is filled with just about all the forces that are against good; therefore, when our children marry spouses of such an environment, we should not have to ask the outcome.

Domestic violence shelters, programs, education centers have been set up all around the world for every class, color, culture, and creed to control this venomous beast.

The national coalition against domestic violence believes that in the near future there will be some progressive legislation in many states to help deal with the violence.

Many other agencies, including the mental health services in some parts of the world, have taken on the challenge of assisting children that have been exposed to domestic violence.

Steps are being taken to provide services in all areas of life to the victims of domestic violence as well as more research being done to empower the court in dealing with the offenders.

In spite of all the efforts to control and conquer domestic violence, one can almost say it will be a long time before our society gets there. The reason is that our society everywhere has become so liberal that it seems as though respect on a whole is slowly moving away from us and reverence and respect are put back stage.

Will domestic violence get conquered in the long run? Yes, it will, but with the help of a society that is able to conquer their individual behavior and habits by their change of heart.

Conclusion

The journey to conquer domestic violence may take some time, but with commitment and dedication, the goal can be achieved. This goal is not to be ignored or taken for granted, for domestic violence, if ignored, will meet every family at their door in some form or fashion

Some of the cultures that have dealt lightly with it for a long time have now realized how real it is and how much it has the power to rob honest, faithful, and loyal people of the real joy and purpose of life. It is a beast and must be dealt with, but it's not a beast by itself. It uses men and women who become perpetrators and offenders and who must also pay the full price for their cruel actions. It brings victimization to the well-being of its victims and must be conquered, for every human being must enjoy their lives in relationship and demolish fear and sickness that is put upon the race by domestic violence. Is there something that could be done to be more cautious?

There are several things mentioned in the book that could be done, but the most important thing that anyone could do is to pray to GOD to help them to choose the right person in their life. If you do so, he will help you, and his choice will be the right choice.

CPSIA information can be obtained at www.ICGtesting.com
Printed in the USA
BVOW08s1253131013

333539BV00001B/9/P